MW00617408

Praise for *How to Lead Nonprofits*

"Many go into nonprofit leadership unprepared for the twin demands of business management and measurable social impact. Finally, we have a resource that guides the way. Nick Grono's masterful *How to Lead Nonprofits* is a book I will be recommending for years to come."

—Arthur C. Brooks, Professor, Harvard Kennedy School and Harvard Business School, and #1 *New York Times* Bestselling Author, *Strength to Strength*

"In *How to Lead Nonprofits*, Nick Grono has accomplished the rare feat of blending intellectual clarity with practical guidance. He lays out a clear and compelling road map for social sector leadership, enlivened with vivid examples and strong writing. This work can help any nonprofit CEO who seeks to transform inspired purpose into a powerful flywheel of tangible impact."

—Jim Collins, *New York Times* Bestselling Author, *Good to Great* and *Good to Great and the Social Sectors*

"Nick Grono reflects on years of nonprofit leadership to produce a book that is timely, thoughtful, and necessary. There is a level of candor and vulnerability that makes it relatable to anyone who is in or aspires to nonprofit leadership in a way that corporate leadership books don't. At a time when the complexity of the external world reverberates through nonprofits, this is a book that nonprofit leaders can find solace in."

—Tirana Hassan, Executive Director, Human Rights Watch

"There is a real need for a practitioner-focused handbook for nonprofit leaders. Nick's book more than meets this need. Informed by Nick's decades of experience in the sector, *How to Lead Nonprofits* provides a very practical road map for leaders of all types of nonprofits, even with the complex range of challenges they face. I recommend this book to all leaders seeking to make a change in the world."

—Cindy McCain, Executive Director, World Food Programme

"This is an important book for anyone looking to build nonprofit institutions that create enduring change. Nick understands the power of using the tools of business to create outsized impact in the social sector. Based on his lived experience, he powerfully outlines what it means both to build and to lead nonprofit organizations."

—Jacqueline Novogratz, Founder and CEO, Acumen

"Drawing on the insights and practical knowledge garnered over his decades leading global nonprofit organizations, Nick Grono shares how nonprofit leaders can aim high and make an impact by focusing on the people and purpose that drive them. This book is an invaluable road map for any nonprofit executive looking to hone their skills and chart an effective path forward."

—Darren Walker, President, Ford Foundation

"Leading a nonprofit organization is a complex juggling act, requiring the balancing of a group's mission with the concerns of staff, partners, and funders. Few manage the challenge better than Nick Grono. Having helped to lead two important global organizations with extraordinary effectiveness, he is well placed to offer guidance on excellence in nonprofit leadership. This book is a valuable and much-needed contribution."

—Kenneth Roth, Executive Director (1993–2022),
Human Rights Watch

"There have been a lot of questions on the nonprofit model, and those of us who have had to navigate it understand its complexity but don't always have the words to explain it. This book helps in giving clarity to leaders and those interested in learning how to succeed in leading nonprofits. It will be a great companion to leaders like me."

—Sophie Otiende, CEO, Global Fund to End Modern Slavery,
and Cofounder, Azadi Kenya

"Every leader who wants to make a real difference in the world should read this book. Nick is not only a highly successful nonprofit CEO but also always curious, keen to explore, open to improvement, and eager to learn from others. In this valuable book, he shares key learnings from his decades-long leadership experience and vast expertise in change-making—to help us make the change that is so urgently needed."

—Mabel van Oranje, Founder and Leader, the European Council on
Foreign Relations and Girls Not Brides, and Serial Social Entrepreneur

"As a newish CEO, this is such a precious book to have on one's table . . . Every chapter blends in so well it's hard to read one in isolation—take note, read it all. It should serve as a useful reference point in your journey as an executive. Keep it on your desk; there'll be a line in there that will provide a great *aha* moment and some relief that being CEO is as rewarding as the challenges you might confront."

—Dr. Comfort Ero, President and CEO,
International Crisis Group

HOW TO
LEAD
NONPROFITS

HOW TO LEAD
NONPROFITS

Turning Purpose into Impact
to Change the World

NICK GRONO

Matt Holt Books
An Imprint of BenBella Books, Inc.
Dallas, TX

Matt Holt is an imprint of BenBella Books, Inc.
10440 N. Central Expressway
Suite 800
Dallas, TX 75231
benbellabooks.com
Send feedback to feedback@benbellabooks.com

BenBella and *Matt Holt* are federally registered trademarks.

Printed in the United States of America
10 9 8 7 6 5 4 3 2 1

Library of Congress Control Number: 2023054053
ISBN 9781637745199 (hardcover)
ISBN 9781637745205 (electronic)

Editing by Katie Dickman
Copyediting by Michael Fedison
Proofreading by Lisa Story and Denise Pangia
Text design and composition by PerfecType, Nashville, TN
Cover design by Brigid Pearson
Printed by Lake Book Manufacturing

To Sarah, Elza, Zoya, Cicely, and Darcey

CONTENTS

INTRODUCTION

On a bleak midwinter's day in London a decade ago, I became the CEO of a brand-new nonprofit organization. I had landed in England the day before from my home country of Australia and was struggling to adjust to the subzero temperature after the blazing sun of the southern summer. It wasn't the only change I was adjusting to.

At this early stage it seemed a little grandiose even to call myself CEO, given I was the sole staff member of my nascent organization, the Freedom Fund. We had no office, no board, no strategic plan, and no programs in place. But what I did bring with me was more than ten years of leadership experience of US and international nonprofits, and another decade before that working in corporate law, government, and banking. I also had a deep belief in the power of well-led nonprofits, with motivated teams, to drive outsized change.

In contrast to its modest circumstances, the Freedom Fund's ambitions were huge: to mobilize the knowledge, capital, and will needed to end modern slavery. Modern slavery is an umbrella term for horrendous crimes such as sex trafficking, forced labor, bonded labor, and forced marriage. It traps fifty million women, men, and children today into lives of violence and extreme exploitation and generates hundreds of billions of dollars in profit every year for its perpetrators. It's also a crime that touches all of us, as countless everyday products—from mobile phones to cotton T-shirts to processed seafood—are produced with forced labor.

The Fund had one big advantage from the beginning, and that was the backing of three highly regarded philanthropic foundations. Thankfully, they were willing to take a bet on this vision and my leadership by providing generous start-up capital to test whether the Fund could make real progress against its ambitious goals.

So, on that cold, gray January day, I had two priorities. The first was to get the basic operational pieces in place so that I could start hiring staff and setting up programs. This meant I had to prepare an initial budget, find an office, draft a work plan for the first year, ensure board members were appointed, and hold the first board meeting.

The bigger—and, to my mind, more important—priority was to use the first few months to put in place the fundamentals that would give the Freedom Fund the best chance of success over the longer term. I was acutely conscious that the start-up funding gave us the opportunity to be deliberate about our purpose, impact, and culture from the very beginning. I was determined not to waste that gift. I wanted to use all that I had learned from my previous decade in the nonprofit world, and my time before that in the private and government sectors, to position the Freedom Fund for success. I was also determined to draw on the wisdom of the many outstanding leaders I had worked with over the years, and the lessons I had absorbed from other impactful nonprofits over that time.

———

Fast-forward to the present. Today the Freedom Fund works in twelve countries, including many of those with the highest burden of modern slavery, such as Brazil, Ethiopia, and Myanmar. We have a global team of eighty-two people. We have partnered with, and helped shift power and resources to, some 150 grassroots organizations. Working with those partners, we have helped bring over 31,000 people out of slavery. Our programs have directly touched the lives of 1.5 million people in slavery or at high risk of it. And they have positively changed the systems affecting more than seven million vulnerable people, reducing their risk of being harmed.

Look beyond those numbers and picture the women and girls who are no longer being exploited in brothels or cotton spinning mills or coerced into marriage; men and boys who are no longer being forced to work in dangerous mines, brick kilns, or fishing boats; women, men, and children who have been helped to escape a myriad of other deeply exploitative situations. To fuel this impact, we have raised over $220 million in funding. Our budget has grown at a rate of about 25 percent year over year, and we have managed this while also recording a very high level of staff satisfaction.

Though we are still a young organization, our work is beginning to garner international attention: Harvard Business School is teaching a case study on the Freedom Fund's strategy and impact. Thought leaders in philanthropy, such as Bridgespan, the Gates Foundation, MacKenzie Scott, and The Philanthropy Workshop, are highlighting the impact of our work. All of this drives our flywheel, enabling us to mobilize more resources and increase our impact.

So how did we get here? The answer is: by focusing relentlessly and with discipline on our purpose and impact. This focus shapes everything the Freedom Fund does. It sets our direction of travel. It helps us build a highly effective organization, enabling us to recruit and retain an out-standing team that shares an inclusive and impact-focused culture. And it ensures we maintain close partnerships with those who have the greatest stake in our success—particularly local communities and courageous grassroots organizations, but also our funders and peer organizations.

WHAT DO SUCCESSFUL NONPROFITS HAVE IN COMMON?

I've spent a lot of time studying successful nonprofits to identify their shared attributes. In addition to my two decades working for nonprofits,

I've also served on seven nonprofit boards to date, which has given me a firsthand perspective on governance.* I also have experience working for business and government: In addition to my early years as a corporate lawyer, I worked at the investment bank Goldman Sachs and later was chief of staff to the Australian attorney general. I spent a number of years providing leadership training to young women and men on a sail-training ship. After some twenty years of leadership, I am increasingly asked to advise and coach other nonprofit leaders, and I've learned a lot from these rich discussions.

All of this has shaped my thinking on what great nonprofit leadership is. The starting point is to identify what the most successful nonprofits have in common. Once we identify this, we can explore the leader's role in building and sustaining these organizations.

Nonprofits come in many forms. They are service-delivery organizations, advocacy organizations, charities, foundations, non-governmental organizations (NGOs), religious organizations, social welfare organizations, and education and arts institutions. There are more than 1.5 million registered nonprofits in the US and millions more globally. Given this diversity, it's not surprising that many factors contribute to nonprofit success—starting with leadership, but also including staff, culture, the issue being addressed, operational context, funding models, and peers and competitors.

But all highly successful nonprofits put purpose and impact at the very heart of everything they do, and they maintain a disciplined and relentless focus on them. Nonprofits exist to make a positive change in

---

* I served first on the board of the Sail Training Association of Western Australia (see the Purpose section in this book) in the 1990s. I've since served on the boards of Crisis Action (as chair), Girls Not Brides, the Jo Cox Foundation (as chair), and Transparentem. I currently serve on the advisory board of Global Witness, a passionate and powerful campaigning organization that takes on governments and companies to protect human rights and secure the future of our planet. I'm also a member of the human-trafficking advisory council of the US-based McCain Institute, founded by former Senator John McCain and Ambassador Cindy McCain.

our world. This is their purpose, their reason for existence. Their contribution to that change is their impact. They save lives, protect rights, tackle poverty and hunger, promote the arts, provide education and health services to the world's least fortunate, and much more. Some nonprofits have more impact than others, and definitions of "positive change" can vary widely, but all have purpose and impact as the golden thread running through all their work.

The power of this approach can best be seen by comparing nonprofits with businesses. Businesses exist to maximize value for their shareholders—that is their principal purpose and how their impact is measured by their shareholders. Successful businesses are defined primarily by their financial returns. Some may have a secondary purpose of doing public good, but financial considerations reign supreme, and that strongly shapes their leadership and differentiates it in important ways from nonprofit leadership.* By contrast, the most effective nonprofits start and end with a focus on change—and understanding this is key to understanding nonprofit leadership.

THE ROLE OF THE LEADER

Given this focus on driving change, what is the role of the leader in building and sustaining great nonprofits? Many (particularly business leaders) argue that the key is to lead nonprofits more like

---

* B Corporations are notable exceptions to this model of profit-driven company. They are for-profit companies that meet the highest standards of social and environmental performance, transparency, and accountability. Effectively, they are mission-driven companies that balance purpose and profit. To become a B Corp, companies must go through an extensive certification process. There are over six thousand certified B Corporations in more than eighty countries and over 150 industries. To learn more, see "What's Behind the B," B Lab website, accessed July 18, 2023, https://usca.bcorporation.net/about-b-corps/; Suntae Kim, Matthew J. Karlesky, Christopher G. Myers, and Todd Schifeling, "Why Companies Are Becoming B Corporations," *Harvard Business Review*, June 17, 2016, https://hbr.org/2016/06/why-companies-are-becoming-b-corporations.

businesses, but this entirely misses the point. The simple fact of leading a profit-driven organization does not, of itself, make you a good leader. There are well-led businesses and badly run ones, just like there are great nonprofits and mediocre ones. One of the world's leading experts on business leadership, Jim Collins, highlighted this by subtitling his study on nonprofit leadership: "why business thinking is not the answer."

Rather, the role of the leader is to harness the power of purpose and use it to shape everything the organization does—internally with its people and externally with its partners—to deliver the greatest possible change.

The framework I use in this book reflects this approach. It is structured around purpose, people, and partners:

Purpose determines a nonprofit's direction of travel and destination. It explains why a nonprofit exists and what it hopes to achieve. The first section of this book will explore "purpose" in detail and the way it shapes mission, impact, and strategy, with a chapter on each.

People are central to the success of any organization. The second section of this book looks internally, at the people and dynamics that power a nonprofit. It starts with a chapter on the CEO's priorities and style. Next comes a chapter on teams—specifically culture and staffing—followed by one on diversity, equity, and inclusion (DEI). The section ends with a chapter on another key group of people, namely your board.

Partners are key to amplifying a nonprofit's impact. Nonprofits have a range of groups with an interest in their success: these are their external stakeholders or, as I prefer to call them, their partners. The book's final section looks at the role of these partners. It starts with a chapter on the individuals and communities you serve, as these are the principal reason for your organization's existence. Next come your funders, who provide the financial fuel on which your organization depends. The last chapter is on collaboration and networks.

At the end of each chapter, I've compiled a short list of "action points." Think of them as a succinct summary of the chapter and the key takeaways.

WHY THIS BOOK?

In writing this book, I was conscious that there is no shortage of literature on leadership. But almost all of it is about running businesses. And, while much of what is written about profit-driven leadership is relevant to nonprofits, there are fundamental differences between the two types of organizations, which means that business literature and experience will never be sufficient to address the needs of nonprofit leaders. This is why successful business leaders can do poorly in leading nonprofits, and why effective nonprofit leaders can stumble when they try and move to private-sector leadership positions.

Despite these differences or, rather, because of them, I regularly compare business and nonprofit practice throughout this book. The contrast illustrates how different incentives lead to different priorities and outcomes, and better shapes our understanding of nonprofit leadership.

There are some very good, and weighty, academic books about nonprofit leadership and the attributes of successful nonprofits. But being largely academic in their approach, they tend to be of limited use to the busy nonprofit leader looking for clear and practical advice on strengthening their leadership and organization.*

How to Lead Nonprofits is written specifically for that busy nonprofit leader, be they a CEO, executive director, board chair, prospective leader,

---

* The exception that proves the rule is the excellent monograph on nonprofit leadership by the leading business researcher and author Jim Collins, titled *Good to Great and the Social Sectors: Why Business Thinking Is Not the Answer* (London, England: Random House Business Books, 2006)—a text I have returned to repeatedly in my nonprofit career.

or aspirational one. For convenience, I will often refer to the CEO, but the intended audience is broader than that.*

Throughout the book, I have drawn heavily on my own experiences over the last twenty years. In so doing, I'm conscious that those experiences have been strongly influenced by the fact that I'm a middle-class white man who has spent most of his working life in the US, UK, Europe, and Australia. So, in addition to referring to the relevant literature, I have also sought out the wisdom of a number of outstanding nonprofit leaders from around the world that I've had the joy of working and collaborating with over the years. My hope is that collectively we can help other nonprofit leaders accelerate some of the learning process and more effectively build impactful and inclusive organizations.

This is meant to be the kind of book I would have found helpful when I started working in nonprofit leadership roles. I've aimed to keep the text short and practical. While the book is structured around the framework of purpose, people, and partners, the chapters are all free-standing. So, if you are more focused on, say, culture than mission, feel free to dive straight into the relevant chapter. The book is intended to be a resource that you can use as and when it suits you. And I don't expect you to agree with everything I have to say—my approach is not to be prescriptive but rather to provide an informed perspective against which you can form your own views.

In short, my objective is to provide you with the tools to become a great nonprofit leader as you strive to make the world a better place.

---

* Leaders of nonprofits are often called CEO or executive director, and sometimes president and CEO. I'll generally use CEO in this book.

PURPOSE

Set the Direction

Let us make our future now, and let us make our dreams tomorrow's reality.

—Malala Yousafzai[1]

I was twenty years old the first time I worked for a nonprofit, though I didn't think of it as such at the time. The "nonprofit" took the form of a 180-foot tall ship, with three masts, sixteen sails, and fifty-five crew members—it was a bit like the pirate ships of old. The ship was called the *Leeuwin* and was run by the Sail Training Association of Western Australia (STAWA).* We would take forty high school and university-age, often disadvantaged, youth out for ten-day ocean voyages during which they would confront challenges ranging from howling gales to seasickness to cramped communal cabins. They would be trained to work as

---

* Now called Leeuwin Ocean Adventure Foundation.

teams (called "watches"), to build confidence, character, and leadership skills. I volunteered during my holidays. I was a "watch-leader," in charge of one of those teams, and part of the ship's leadership. The experience was often transformative for those who participated. It certainly was for me, given the responsibility of leading teams of eight to ten young people at an early age.

I was keen to contribute more to the work of the organization, so, a few years after I first sailed on the *Leeuwin*, I became a board member of STAWA. I had recently qualified as a lawyer, and my hope was to contribute to the organization's governance. This was my first real introduction to nonprofit leadership. The organization's declared purpose was to "enrich the lives of young people," and it aimed to do this through "adventure, participation, and the challenge of sailing a purpose-built Tall Ship."[2] Like so many small nonprofits (this one had a full-time staff of eight, along with an army of volunteers), it was focused on keeping the doors open and serving the youth of Western Australia. We had a mission statement and a fairly straightforward strategy, though it wasn't written down in the form of a strategic plan. We measured impact by counting how many young people sailed on the *Leeuwin* each year, with lots of anecdotal stories of individual transformation.

STAWA's approach to strategy and impact measurement was rudimentary. But the organization was always true to its purpose of enriching the lives of young people. And it was always clear on how it would do that—through the adventure of sailing on a tall ship. As a result, STAWA has had a deep and lasting impact on over forty thousand young people who have sailed on the *Leeuwin* over the last thirty-five years. It's also become an important part of the social fabric of Fremantle, the port town where it is based. My experiences with Leeuwin and STAWA are my nonprofit North Star, always reminding me that when purpose and impact are at the heart of a nonprofit, its work can transform lives.

Because nonprofits pursue positive change rather than financial returns, they have developed other concepts to guide what they do and how—namely, vision, purpose, mission, and impact. These concepts all derive from the organization's purpose, i.e., its reason for existence. Nonprofits usually have an overarching vision—the long-term picture of what they'd like to achieve. Their mission is the action they take to fulfill their purpose and achieve their vision. Their impact is the positive change they contribute to in pursuit of their purpose. Their strategy is their practical road map to turning their purpose into impact. And all of these elements are usually pulled together in a strategic plan.

The leader's role is to ensure that the organization's purpose is powerfully reflected in its mission, impact, and strategy, and that's what we will explore in this section. As Dina Sherif, CEO of the Legatum Center at MIT, put it to me, "Know your organization's purpose. That will always be your lifeline."[3]

While this discussion can sometimes seem a little technical, understanding these concepts is important because, properly applied, they set organizations on the path to achieving the greatest possible impact.

CHAPTER 1

Mission

Be Clear About the Work

> *A small body of determined spirits fired by an unquenchable*
> *faith in their mission can alter the course of human history.*
> —Mahatma Gandhi[1]

Staying true to mission requires nonprofits to maintain constant focus. Even the most professional ones sometimes get sidetracked, as I experienced during my time with the International Crisis Group ("Crisis Group").

Crisis Group is one of the world's preeminent conflict prevention organizations. Its purpose is to prevent and resolve deadly conflicts. Established during the Balkans war in the 1990s by foreign policy experts appalled at the failure of the international community to respond effectively to such a brutal conflict, it quickly earned a reputation for its impactful mission—producing deeply knowledgeable and nuanced policy-focused reports from analysts based in the conflict zones they covered, combined with high-level advocacy to Western policymakers. Its board of former senior government officials and policymakers—which over the years have included several Nobel Peace laureates and scores of former prime ministers and foreign ministers—helped it get access to the right decision-makers.

From its early years, Crisis Group covered the civil wars in Sudan, including in Darfur, where mass atrocities were being committed against the region's non-Arab population. As former US Secretary of State Colin Powell noted, "In Darfur . . . International Crisis Group was ringing the alarm bell . . . They gave us insight. We didn't always agree with them. It's not their role to come into agreement with us. It's their role to reflect ground truth."[2]

In 2006, a bold new US human rights foundation, Humanity United, launched an activist campaign to pressure US policymakers to do more to prevent genocide and other mass atrocities, with a particular focus on the war in Darfur. The foundation called this campaign the Enough Project and backed it with an $8 million grant over five years. The campaign would involve a partnership between Crisis Group (providing field-based research and analysis) and the DC-based think tank Center for American Progress (providing US advocacy expertise).[3]

Crisis Group gratefully accepted its sizable share of the grant without fully thinking through how the campaign would fit with its mission, and the Enough Project launched in March 2007. At the time, I was vice president of Crisis Group with overall responsibility for our operations, including advocacy and fundraising. Dazzled by the generosity of the grant, on an issue we were deeply engaged in, we did not consider whether conducting grassroots activism was consistent with our core focus on complex policy formulation and advocacy to high-level policymakers.

As quickly became apparent, it was not. In fact, the situation was a textbook case of mission creep. Activist campaigning requires clear and strident calls for action—such as imposing a no-fly zone (the enforcement of which requires the shooting down of the target country's military planes, and which effectively amounts to a declaration of war)—aimed at mobilizing concerned members of the public. In contrast, high-level policy advocacy usually requires a more nuanced articulation of the drivers of the conflict and the ways to influence them, directly targeting policymakers and other officials. Both are critically important, but they don't always work easily together, and certainly not when coming from the same organization. Moreover, our close involvement in the activist campaign was undermining the effectiveness of our advocacy to high-level policymakers, who were confused by the mixed messages. It was also causing discord within Crisis Group, particularly with some of our experts on the ground in Africa who fundamentally disagreed with much of the activist messaging. While we understood public-facing activism to be critical to political change, we came to realize that we weren't the right organization to be doing it. The Enough campaigning was dragging us off mission.

We decided that this could only be resolved by recommitting to our core mission of high-level advocacy. In May 2007, we agreed to part ways with the Enough Project.[4] The staff leading that work left to work for Center for American progress, before setting up their own organization—and all the funding moved with them. The transition was not straightforward, and there was a degree of unhappiness on the part of those staff leaving, and at Humanity United, which stopped funding Crisis Group for a number of years. That said, the longer-term outcome was that Crisis Group returned to a laser-like focus on what it did best, and the Enough Project became a highly successful and impactful organization in its own right, under the leadership of my former colleague John Prendergast and with the high-profile backing of committed celebrity activists such as George Clooney and Don Cheadle. And, over time, we rebuilt a strong and productive relationship with Humanity United.

Understanding mission is key to understanding nonprofits. While purpose is their "why," mission is their "how." Nonprofits are often called "mission-driven" organizations because success is judged on their impact in delivering their mission. Much follows from this framing, especially when it comes to working out whether the organization is achieving its desired change.

But understanding a nonprofit's mission can be challenging. Too often what an organization actually does—its mission—diverges from what it says it does in its written, public-facing mission statement. This leads to confusion when comparing the statement with the actual work.

So, in this chapter, I'll explain what we mean by mission and how it relates to an organization's purpose and vision. We will then look at how mission shapes a nonprofit's impact. And finally, we'll look at how to ensure the mission statement properly reflects your nonprofit's purpose and mission.

HOW VISION, PURPOSE, AND MISSION RELATE TO EACH OTHER

An organization's *vision* is invariably aspirational, such as "a world free of poverty." Some organizations define and publish their vision, but many don't.* A nonprofit's *purpose* is a broad statement of how it intends to contribute to the world it envisions.† Its *mission* is more specific, setting out what the organization does, and for whom; i.e., the action it takes to achieve its purpose.

---

* There can be a fine line between an organization's vision and an ambitious purpose, which is probably why many nonprofits don't bother to define their vision.

† The best statements of purpose "begin with a verb (like 'reduce' or 'protect' or 'make') and then a description of the problem you want to address or the conditions you want to foster." Alison Green and Jerry Hauser, *Managing to Change the World* (Washington, DC: The Management Center, 2009), 61.

KEY TERMS

Vision: the desired future state, usually aspirational, e.g., "a world free of poverty"

Purpose: the organization's reason for being; how it intends to contribute to the world it envisions, e.g., "to empower the poor to realize their potential and to break out of the vicious cycle of poverty"[*]

Mission: the action an organization takes to fulfill its purpose, e.g., "providing comprehensive financial services" to the poor[5]

Mission statement: a succinct written statement of the organization's purpose and mission

Strategy: the set of decisions and trade-offs a nonprofit needs to make to achieve the greatest impact in pursuit of its purpose

Strategic plan: the written strategy; it may be a short framework for decision-making, a long document with detailed multi-year plans for every aspect of the organization's work over the next three to five years or longer, or something in between

Purpose and mission are often used interchangeably in written mission statements, but it helps to understand the difference when defining what your organization does.

The purpose of the Girl Scouts of the USA is to "build girls of courage, confidence, and character, who make the world a better place." Its mission is to empower girls to "discover the fun, friendship, and power

---

[*] This is the purpose of Grameen Bank, based in Bangladesh, which received the Nobel Peace Prize in 2006 jointly with its founder, Muhammad Yunus. See "Vision and Mission," Grameen Bank website, accessed, February 13, 2023, https://grameenbank.org.bd/about/vision-mission.

of girls together. Girls grow courageous and strong through a wide variety of enriching experiences, such as field trips, skill-building sports clinics, community service projects, cultural exchanges, and environmental stewardships."[6]

EDWINS Leadership & Restaurant Institute's purpose is to "change the face of re-entry for formerly incarcerated prisoners" in the US. Its approach to doing this "is three-fold: to teach a skilled and in-demand trade in the culinary arts, empower willing minds through a passion for hospitality management, and prepare students for a successful transition home."[7]

The purpose of More in Common, an impressive community-building organization working in the US and Europe, is "to understand the forces driving us apart, to find common ground and help to bring people together to tackle our shared challenges." And its mission? "We draw from groundbreaking research to test and find solutions, working with partners that have the capacity to make a real difference at scale. And we help build the larger field of efforts to strengthen democratic societies against the threats of polarization and division."[8]

So what about the Freedom Fund? My very first task as the newly appointed CEO of the newly launched organization was to identify what its purpose and mission would be. The three founders, all philanthropic foundations whose representatives were members of our board, agreed on the purpose of the organization and the key challenges but had diverging views on how to address them. They all agreed that the global anti-slavery sector was chronically underresourced; that it was fragmented and needed more collaboration, particularly in countries with the highest burden of slavery; and that the sector was desperately short of robust evidence of which interventions worked best to tackle this hidden crime. Contending with these challenges would be the new organization's purpose.

But the founders differed on the most effective way to do so. One believed the priority was to work on the ground with clusters of local organizations to combat slavery in affected communities in low-income countries. Another thought we could best add value by focusing on industries (such as fishing or fast fashion) that were rife with extreme exploitation. And the third wanted us to link local-level impact and research with its work to influence global and national policymakers.

I was in full agreement on the challenges and comfortable with the diverging views on ways forward. To my mind, we were a start-up. We had to identify two or three potentially powerful ways of working, then test and refine them, and scale those we identified as the most impactful, based on robust evidence.

To reflect all of this in our mission statement, I drafted it in two parts. The first part set out our purpose, the reason the Freedom Fund had been brought into existence and what differentiated it from other anti-slavery organizations. I identified this to be "to mobilize the knowledge, capital and will needed to end slavery."

The second part, setting out the action we would take to achieve this, was expressed as follows:

> We identify and invest in the most effective frontline efforts to eradicate modern slavery in the countries and sectors where it is most prevalent. Partnering with visionary investors, governments, anti-slavery organizations and those at risk of exploitation, we tackle the systems that allow slavery to persist and thrive. Working together, we protect vulnerable populations, liberate and reintegrate those enslaved and prosecute those responsible.

There is school of thought that mission statements need to be short and terse—a few words or a single sentence. This second paragraph was maybe a little longer than is ideal, but I valued being specific about our priorities, so that we could align board members, funders, staff, and partner organizations. Our board agreed and approved this mission statement.

Looking back at the statement many years later, I believe it's still a good reflection of what we do and the impact we are held accountable for achieving, with one key exception. The exception is the leadership of survivors of slavery, which now plays a much more central role in our work and our plans for the future. So, while that is already part of our mission (in that we are already doing it), survivor leadership is not yet included in our mission statement. Given that it's such an important part of the Freedom Fund, it needs to be incorporated, not least because the statement is the public-facing expression of what we do. We'll revise the mission statement when we embark on our next strategic planning process.*

DEFINING A POWERFUL MISSION

Unless you are starting a nonprofit from scratch, your nonprofit is already implementing its mission. By definition, whatever your organization is doing is its mission. If that's a powerful mission—one that is designed to deliver maximum impact in pursuit of your organization's purpose— all is well. As the management guru Peter Drucker stated in his book *Managing the Non-Profit Organization*: "The first thing to talk about is what missions work and what missions don't work and how to define the mission. For the ultimate test is not the beauty of the mission statement. **The ultimate test is right action** [my emphasis] . . . the first job of the leader is to think through and define the mission of the institution."[9]

A powerful mission ensures that your organization has distinctive and intentional impact as it pursues its purpose. It should be credibly ambitious relative to the resources you can reasonably expect to mobilize.

If your mission is modest for the resources you have available, you'll most likely succeed in your mission, but not in achieving the impact you should, given your purpose and resources. Let's assume you run a

---

* I did give thought to updating our mission statement in advance of publication of this book but decided that highlighting that it was a little out of date was better reflective of our reality, and that of many other nonprofits.

nonprofit committed to tackling homelessness in San Francisco [purpose] by running a high-quality twenty-person shelter for the homeless in a rapidly gentrifying part of the city [mission], and you have an endowment of millions of dollars. You may well run the shelter very effectively, at full capacity, and provide world-class services to the twenty people who can access your shelter at any one time. Strictly speaking, this would amount to success given your mission to run the shelter. But it's not a powerful mission. Your nonprofit won't be having the impact on homelessness in San Francisco that its purpose and funding suggest it should. It won't be delivering the scale of change it should be capable of delivering.

If your mission is overly ambitious, you may fail to achieve it while still having a great deal of impact, or you could just end up being demoralized by your failure to carry it out. Take the same San Francisco–based nonprofit. Assume its mission is now to tackle homelessness by opening shelters across the city, working with the homeless it serves to develop ambitious policy recommendations to the state and local governments and advocate for change, with $1 million in annual income. Chances are it will struggle to achieve this mission, at least in the short term, given its big ambitions and limited resources. That could be demoralizing, or it could be a powerful motivation to raise more money and support to make a real difference to homelessness in that city. Your leadership and strategy will help determine that.

If your mission is not defined in a way to deliver maximum impact for the resources you can expect to mobilize, you should revise it. It may be that the organization started with a strong mission and clarity about what it was doing, but over time has engaged in mission creep, taking on projects not because they aligned closely to the mission, but because there was a willing funder or an interesting opportunity (as illustrated by the opening story in this chapter). To take another example, imagine that a donor came to the San Francisco homelessness nonprofit and offered it funding to run a shelter in neighboring Oakland. Taking that on would be a classic example of mission creep—unless the nonprofit decided to revise and expand its mission and strategy to run shelters in, say, the wider Bay Area (including Oakland), with a credible plan to do this well. Mission creep is a constant threat for nonprofits. Only strong leadership and a commitment to the core mission can resist the forces trying to pull you off course.

There are other reasons your organization may have drifted from its mission. You may have started initiatives and realized they were not closely aligned to what you wanted to do or to the key populations you want to serve but kept on with them because of opposition from donors and staff to pulling out. Or your board is divided and pulling you in different directions. Or you started with a very modest mission, and haven't revisited it even though it clearly wasn't designed to achieve the change you are aiming for. The end result will likely be that your organization is unfocused and distracted and not having the impact it should.

How do you assess if your current mission is fit for purpose? Start with the fundamentals. Picture what you would do if you were starting the organization from scratch, with current resources, and a blank sheet for your mission. Knowing what you know, how can you have maximum impact in pursuit of your purpose? Ask staff, the people and communities you serve, and other stakeholders. Do they have a clear and shared idea of what the organization should be doing? Do they think you are making the best use of the resources available to you? Is the organization focused or scattershot? Is it making a meaningful difference?

If your conclusion is that your existing mission is significantly off track, then you need to do some serious work to get the organization back on track. That may require a major review of your strategy, and some painful course correction—but good leaders will lean into this if they determine the mission is not fit for purpose, as it's the only way to position the organization for maximum impact. We'll look at this more deeply in the chapter on strategy.

THE MISSION SETS EXPECTATIONS FOR IMPACT

One consequence of measuring nonprofit impact against mission is that it is difficult to compare the performance of one nonprofit with that of another. This is one key way in which nonprofits differ from businesses. Since success for a business is largely determined by its financial returns, performance can be compared much more easily. Hence, Google's performance can be readily compared against that of peers, such as Facebook or Microsoft, or even against companies in a completely different sector of the global economy, such as Walmart or Goldman Sachs or Ford. While fundamental differences between these organizations exist, the companies can all be broadly compared, based on their financial returns to shareholders. This is what drives their decision-making and accountability to their shareholders.

But nonprofits don't have a sole, simple metric by which their performance can be compared. For a start, they don't have owners or shareholders as such. And their outcomes range from lives saved, children educated, justice advanced, arts promoted, ideas generated—all of which are difficult to measure, let alone compare. Even between two organizations working on similar issues, say, addressing child poverty in Houston, it can be very difficult to compare impact and performance, as the organizations may have divergent views on the ways they want to tackle poverty and the outcomes they seek. For example, one may focus on school meals and the other on advocacy to local officials. Usually, the best we can do is ensure our nonprofit has a powerful and clearly defined mission and that it is executing successfully against it. At worst, it means ineffective or badly led nonprofits can operate for many years without being held accountable for their lack of performance.

But, whether or not we can robustly compare the performance of nonprofits, committed leaders must always be seeking ways to assess how effective their organization is. They cannot hold themselves accountable to their stakeholders—first, the people they serve, but funders, board members, and staff too—if they cannot credibly assess what progress their organization has made. We'll explore this in the next chapter, on impact.

THE MISSION STATEMENT COMES LAST

Once you are clear on your purpose and mission, you can communicate them through your mission statement. A mission statement is usually drafted when an organization is first founded, and then reviewed periodically, usually every few years when your organization embarks on a new strategic planning process. You'll often find the statement in an organization's strategic plan, and perhaps on its website.

Many experts place a lot of weight on the mission statement. They say things like: "A clear and well-focused mission statement can serve to guide all major decisions that a nonprofit organization must make—especially decisions about which new programs and projects to undertake, which to avoid, and which to exit."*

While that may be aspirational, I don't think it reflects the reality of most nonprofits. For my part, I'm more interested in "right action" than what the mission statement says the organization does. Missions often evolve more quickly than the mission statement. Of course, ideally, the two align, but frequently the mission statement gets left behind, particularly with rapidly growing nonprofits. In fact, in most organizations, you will probably find that it's only the CEO who regularly reviews the mission statement (and perhaps not even the CEO). For most staff, it

---

* See Kim Jonker and William F. Meehan III, "Mission Matters Most," *Stanford Social Innovation Review*, February 19, 2014. They go further in this and an earlier article, "Curbing Mission Creep," *Stanford Social Innovation Review*, Winter 2008, and outline "the seven characteristics of a well-honed statement of mission: It is focused. It solves unmet public needs. It leverages unique skills. It guides trade-offs. It inspires, and is inspired by, key stakeholders. It anticipates change. And it sticks in memory." This is a lot for a mission statement to deliver.

is also the CEO who will have shaped their understanding of the mission, by talking about it and making clear what is and what isn't part of the mission. Their understanding will also be molded by the day-to-day work of the organization, by decisions on which programs to start or not, and by how impact is measured—not just by what is set out in the statement. All of this underscores the importance of the CEO intentionally shaping the organization's understanding of the evolving mission and ensuring that it is internalized by staff. The CEO has the primary responsibility to hold and expound on the vision, purpose, and mission of an organization.

CASE STUDY

Drumming Home the Mission

Crisis Group provides a clear example of how a leader can make the mission real to staff. When I joined the organization, and for many years after, we didn't have a written strategic plan. But staff at Crisis Group had a clearer understanding of its purpose and mission than any I have come across before or since. And that was because the then CEO, Gareth Evans, was relentless about explaining what the organization did, and, just as importantly, what it did not do. Its purpose was to prevent and resolve deadly conflict, and its mission was to carry out field-based research, publish nuanced analysis and reports, and engage in high-level advocacy to policymakers and those who influenced them. That's all quite wordy, but Gareth would repeatedly highlight that we had analysts based on the ground in conflict-affected countries, not on the other side of the world in Washington, DC, or London. He would constantly hammer home the need for expert analysis, with clear and practical recommendations, not idealistic statements of what might be nice to happen.

And he would make it very clear what Crisis Group would not do, such as big "documentation" exercises to record atrocities, for example, as those were better left to organizations that specialized in that work. He would talk about our mission internally at staff meetings and retreats and externally at public events. As a result, there was a clear and shared understanding by staff and key external actors about what Crisis Group did and didn't do, and that gave great focus to our work. And when we occasionally strayed, as with the Enough Project, we quickly course-corrected.*

None of this is to say you shouldn't have a mission statement. A written statement is helpful, provided it accurately reflects your purpose and mission, and it can play a key role in fundraising and communications efforts. But, to my mind, your first priority is to engage in doing what needs to be done to advance your purpose, rather than get unduly focused on whether a proposed activity fits your statement or not. The statement should reflect the actual mission, not vice versa. If there is a mismatch, you need to work out whether you've drifted from what you should be doing—so your mission needs to be revised—or you have evolved from what your mission statement says you do, in which case the statement needs to be updated.

---

* Crisis Group does now have a written mission statement. Its purpose is to work "to prevent wars and shape policies that will build a more peaceful world." And its mission: "Crisis Group sounds the alarm to prevent deadly conflict. We build support for the good governance and inclusive politics that enable societies to flourish. We engage directly with a range of conflict actors to seek and share information, and to encourage intelligent action for peace." International Crisis Group website, accessed May 23, 2023, https://www.crisisgroup.org/who-we-are.

When you draft or redraft the mission statement, you should succinctly express the organization's purpose and mission.* The statement should set out the problem the organization exists to address or the change it wants to bring about (purpose), and who it serves and how it will achieve the desired change (mission). Ideally it is no more than two or three sentences. The mission statements of Girl Scouts, EDWINS, and More in Common are all good examples.†

An up-to-date statement can be used by the CEO to ensure that all key stakeholders, including your staff, board, and funders, have a shared understanding of the mission.‡ It can also be used to market your organization to potential funders and other external audiences. If your mission statement is well crafted, anyone reading it will know what your nonprofit does and doesn't do and why.

---

* Often a mission statement is simply a statement of purpose, which can be confusing given these are labeled "mission" statements. There is nothing necessarily wrong with limiting your statement to purpose if you are clear about that purpose, though readers will have to look elsewhere for specifics of what you actually do. Too often, however, the description of purpose is too broad to be of any use. For example, CARE USA says its mission is to "work around the globe to save lives, defeat poverty, and achieve social justice." This statement could apply to pretty well any international humanitarian or poverty alleviation organization. It certainly doesn't tell you what CARE actually does, and it won't help you assess whether CARE is successful in what it is doing. It likely doesn't help CARE staff in understanding what they do either.

† On how to write a clear mission statement, see Erica Barnhart, "Great Mission. Bad Statement," *Stanford Social Innovation Review*, January 15, 2016, https://ssir .org/articles/entry/great_mission._bad_statement.

‡ Most organizations put their mission statement on their website. Many describe their purpose and mission in the "About Us" section of their website, without specifically labeling them as such. Mission statements can usually also be found in the opening section of an organization's strategic plan.

If your nonprofit has a powerful mission, reflected in a well-crafted mission statement, and holds itself accountable for its impact against that mission, it will have a strong foundation on which to deliver positive change, as we will see in the next chapter on impact.

MISSION ACTION POINTS

Be Clear About the Work

- Review your organization's purpose and mission.
- Assess whether the mission is credibly ambitious relative to your organization's purpose and the resources you can reasonably expect to mobilize.
- If not, then revise the mission to ensure it is fit for purpose, and reflect that in an updated mission statement.

CHAPTER 2

Impact

Identify and Measure Change

> *A great organization is one that delivers superior performance and makes a distinctive impact over a long period of time.*
>
> —Jim Collins[1]

As soon as the Freedom Fund launched, I started having lively discussions with our new board members on what "impact" meant for the organization. Given we are an anti-slavery organization, one of the first impact goals the board agreed on was a target for "lives liberated" from slavery and trafficking, i.e., how many people we directly helped exit situations of extreme exploitation. This goal has the merit of being a fairly clear metric—in most cases, it's straightforward enough to work out whether someone is in a situation of modern slavery or not. But the problem with a metric like this is that it doesn't really tell us whether we are contributing to a genuine reduction in the levels of slavery and extreme exploitation in the regions where we operate, which is the change we really want to see.

Take a group of villages in northern India where child trafficking is endemic due to desperate poverty, caste and religious discrimination, and weak rule of law. Vulnerable girls are often coerced into domestic servitude or trafficked into brothels, and vulnerable boys are forced to work in brick kilns and stone quarries or factories. Say that over five years, by partnering with local community organizations, we helped liberate five hundred children from trafficking in those villages. That's a big figure and may sound like success. But what if one thousand other children had been trafficked into slavery during that same period, meaning that child trafficking in those villages actually increased? Was that success, failure, or something in between? The overall level of trafficking has increased, but perhaps it would have been even higher if not for our intervention. But if our impact is being evaluated by a measurable reduction in the prevalence of slavery, then clearly this is a failure on that metric.*

All of this goes to show that determining what counts as impact can be challenging. Or rather, there can be various types of impact. If you are liberated from slavery, that certainly is impactful for you and your family. But perhaps not for the community if overall levels of exploitation stay the same, or even increase. The way we agreed with our board to address this is to measure different types of impact—at the individual level, at the community level, and at a broader "systems" level—each with its own target. We've continued measuring in this way since, refining our efforts along the way.

---

* In the Freedom Fund's case, in four years we saw a reduction of over 80 percent in the overall levels of slavery in the communities in which we were working in northern India. See "Unlocking What Works: How Community-Based Interventions Are Ending Bonded Labour in India," September 2019, Freedom Fund website at freedomfund.org/wp-content/uploads/Freedom-Fund-Evidence-in-Practice -Paper-Unlocking-what-works.pdf. The Freedom Fund stopped working in India in January 2023 due to the Indian government placing restrictions on the ability of international organizations to fund community-based organizations in the country.

Every nonprofit I have worked for has had clarity about its purpose and mission and the change it wanted to help bring about. But every one of them, including the Freedom Fund, has struggled to come up with ways to effectively measure just how much progress it was making in achieving that change.

The Sail Training Association of Western Australia could readily count how many young people had taken leadership courses on the *Leeuwin* but, beyond that, struggled to assess the extent to which it had "enriched" their lives, and how many lives it should aim to enrich to fulfill its purpose.

Crisis Group could accurately measure how many reports it published each year on deadly conflict, and how many advocacy meetings it held, but was not able to assess the extent to which it actually influenced policymakers (beyond scattered anecdotal accounts), let alone the extent to which any such influence reduced the occurrence or duration of conflicts.

Girls Not Brides, a nonprofit dedicated to ending child marriage around the world, and on whose board I served for many years, is a membership organization whose mission is to serve its many hundreds of member organizations and to mobilize their collective expertise and power to drive change. But beyond recording how many members it had, it struggled to assess how effectively it contributed to a reduction in child marriage.

The takeaway is not that these organizations were poorly led or ineffective. On the contrary, they are among some of the best-led nonprofits I have come across. Rather, the lesson is that measuring something as potentially amorphous as "change," however defined, can be a real challenge to even the most effective organizations. But it is a challenge leaders need to embrace.

In this chapter we will look at why impact is central to everything nonprofits do. We will explain what impact is and how it differs from other related concepts, such as inputs and activities. We will explore why a better understanding of impact will allow your organization to become more effective in driving the change it seeks to bring about. And we will finish up by confronting some of the obstacles to better understanding and measuring impact.

WHAT IS IMPACT AND WHY IS IT IMPORTANT?

Given the centrality of impact to the work of nonprofits, leaders should ensure that there is a clear understanding throughout their organization of the impact that it seeks to bring about, and how progress will be assessed.

There is often confusion, even among experienced nonprofit leaders, about what is meant by impact and exactly what needs to be measured. As a result, nonprofits often measure the wrong things. Some purport to measure their impact by tracking funds raised or spent on their running costs, the number of members recruited, how many reports they published or conferences they convened, website traffic, or "beneficiaries" served, e.g., with meals, shelter, health, or education services. These may all be useful metrics for operational or programmatic purposes, but they are not good measures of impact, as they are not measures of change. Rather, they are measures of the resources committed to running the organization, i.e., its *overheads* (often called *inputs*) or its *activities* (often called *outputs*).*

The best-in-class way to identify and measure the impact you want to achieve is to focus on the *outcomes* your work has contributed to—i.e., the actual changes that come about after your activities have taken place, such as education levels increased, poverty or vulnerability reduced, rights protected—and then assess the extent to which those outcomes can be linked to your activities.

---

* While the terms "activities" and "outputs" can be used interchangeably, I'll use "activities" throughout to avoid confusion.

Given that impact is such a central concept for nonprofits, I'm going to explore it in some detail. Impact is like financial returns for businesses, and you can be sure that successful business leaders have a very clear idea of what financial returns they are seeking to achieve. They relentlessly measure their business's financial performance, and are assessed on that performance. They also are clear about the difference between a business's inputs (staff costs, research and development, sales and marketing), its activities (goods manufactured, services provided), and its outcomes (financial returns). Successful nonprofit leaders need similar clarity and discipline about the impact they are seeking to achieve.

Even though the focus should be on outcomes (i.e., change), you should still also measure your organization's activities, as this is usually an important first step on the way to measuring outcomes. For a start, if you can't count how many people you have served, students you have taught, or reports you have published, then you probably aren't managing your program well. Or perhaps you are counting these activities, and realize that you're not doing as many things or reaching as many people as you anticipated. That will indicate that your program is unlikely to have the outcomes you were expecting, without you having to go the extra mile and measure those outcomes: if you serve half the meals you anticipated or teach half the students you intended, you probably aren't going to reduce hunger or increase education levels to the extent forecasted. But you shouldn't mistake activities themselves for impact.

EXAMPLES OF NONPROFIT "INPUTS" AND "ACTIVITIES"

Look at the impact statements or annual reports of many nonprofits, and you will often find statements about their inputs, such as fundraising, or their activities. These may be important metrics, but they are not in themselves measures of impact. For example:

- "Millions of volunteers enable 221 million meals to be delivered to 2.4 million seniors each year." —Meals on Wheels America [activities][2]
- "The world's largest platform for social change, with over 329 million users globally." —Change.org [activities][3]
- "Heritage [Foundation] experts appear on television and radio dozens of times each week, publish hundreds of policy research reports annually, and host hundreds of meetings a year with grassroots leaders and local and national officials." —The Heritage Foundation [activities][4]
- "Nearly 85% of our revenue directly benefits our clients. 11% of our revenue is used to operate our programs and only 5% of our revenue is spent on fundraising." —Ali Forney Center [inputs][5]

Examples of *outcomes* include a reduction in homelessness or hunger and improved education and health for the target population. These may be changes for which your organization can claim direct responsibility, like reducing hunger through the provision of meals, improving students' academic performance through tutoring, or stopping evictions through legal support. But you may also contribute to impact that feels more indirect: changes to legislation, changes in cultural norms (e.g., promoting the importance of girls' education in countries where it is not the norm), or otherwise playing a role in shifting complex social, political, or economic systems. (See more on "systems change" later in the chapter.)

Focusing on impact is how your nonprofit holds itself accountable to its key audiences: primarily, those you serve, and your donors and staff. Ideally, you have an idea of the outcomes you want to achieve over, say, three to five years, and you can then set targets and track your progress. Doing so allows you to measure your performance, and it helps you to better allocate resources to achieve the greatest change. However, this is not always possible when you are starting a nonprofit or a new program and don't have enough information to set robust targets. In this case, you may want to set provisional targets, or just measure impact as you go along, until you have a baseline against which to set targets for future years.

In the ideal scenario, you possess a clear and measurable mission, well-defined and -aligned targets for the impact you seek to achieve (directly or indirectly), and the resources necessary to drive your efforts and measure your progress toward those goals. But aligning all three components is genuinely hard. However, even well-positioned nonprofits can do better at setting and measuring goals for and measuring impact. The investment is worthwhile because, done well, your organization will have a greater chance of delivering the change it seeks to bring about.

CASE STUDY

What Great Impact Looks Like

One truly impressive example of nonprofit impact is that of the National Foundation for Infantile Paralysis (NFIP), later rebranded as the March of Dimes, which played a central role in largely eliminating polio in the US.

In the 1930s, polio caused paralysis in hundreds of thousands of victims, mostly children, each year, including thousands in the US alone. The NFIP was founded in 1938 by President Roosevelt, himself an adult victim of polio. Its mission was "to lead, direct, and unify the fight" against polio. Central to NFIP's mission was funding research into a vaccine for polio. Among many other initiatives, NFIP funded the efforts of a young Dr. Jonas Salk to produce a vaccine and then conduct a massive controlled trial on two million children in 1954. Those efforts proved successful, and the Salk vaccine was approved for mass immunization throughout the US in 1955 through a campaign heavily pro-moted by NFIP. Within two years, polio cases had been cut by 90 percent. The disease was largely eliminated in the US by 1961 and fully eliminated there by 1979.

Note that NFIP's mission wasn't to eliminate polio but rather to play a leadership role in the fight against it. NFIP went above and beyond what was already an ambitious mission. This is one of those happy situations where the impact of a nonprofit (working with many other partners, including the US government) well and truly exceeded the expectations set by its big mission.*

THE BENEFITS OF MEASURING IMPACT

Measuring impact effectively can be hard, so you may well ask yourself: Why should we bother when we can get by on measuring activities, such as reports published or meals delivered? Or by preparing selective, feel-good case studies as evidence of impact? Why go the extra mile, especially if it will consume precious funding and staff time? These are fair questions.

Measuring activities is useful, and often a precondition to measuring outcomes, but the investment in measuring your actual impact (i.e., outcomes) can be a force multiplier for your work in a number of ways.

1. Understanding What Works and What Doesn't

When you know what works most effectively, you can allocate your resources accordingly, generating more impact for the funding available.

---

* For more background on March of Dimes, see Georgette Baghdady and Joanne M. Maddock, "Marching to a Different Mission," *Stanford Social Innovation Review*, Spring 2008.

You may decide to reallocate funding to more successful initiatives, or drop or retool initiatives that are not proving as effective. Good evidence gives you the tools to invest your resources more efficiently. This is the most important reason to invest in rigorous impact measurement. Successful businesses have the discipline of the financial bottom line, so are constantly assessing which of their initiatives are profitable and which are not, and adjusting behavior accordingly. Nonprofits should bring a similar discipline to their performance, but based on impact, not profit.

The most effective way to do this, though one that is not always feasible (due to cost or lack of available data), is to get empirical evidence of your impact. With this, you can assess whether your organization's efforts are delivering the change you want to see. Of course, you can rely on anecdotal evidence or your own judgment, but these are not substitutes for rigorous evaluation.

Efforts to eliminate malaria are instructive. Insecticide-treated bednets are known to be effective tools in preventing infection. But experts disagreed over whether nonprofits could better promote the use of bednets among vulnerable populations in Kenya by giving them away or selling them cheaply. Those advocating for selling the nets (for a nominal fee) believed this would screen out those who would not use the nets and increase the likelihood that those who bought them would use them. Yet a randomized control trial* provided clear evidence that the better strategy was to give nets away.[6] Now, based on this research, a number of highly cost-effective nonprofits like Against Malaria Foundation have built their missions around giving away free nets.

---

* A randomized control trial (RCT) is a study that randomly assigns participants to either receive a service or program or to be in a control group, in order to compare the two groups' outcomes. It's regarded as a particularly rigorous way of measuring impact.

2. A Powerful Fundraising Tool

Clear evidence of impact provides validation to your existing donors, and allows you to make a strong case to potential donors. Donors—from members of the public to the largest foundations—want to know that their support will make a difference. In the absence of evidence, we tell them stories and share details of activities. These can be compelling in building engagement, but they are no substitute for evidence of genuine impact.

One of the most important recent trends in philanthropy demonstrates this. Donors have long been resistant to the idea of giving cash to poor individuals in developing countries, instead of, say, providing food or job training or shelter. They worried that support in the form of direct cash payments would cause local prices to rise and stoke resentment from community members who did not receive cash. Underlying these concerns were deeply held and often discriminatory beliefs that poor people don't know how to spend money responsibly and shouldn't be trusted to make their own financial decisions. Over time, evidence built up by early pioneers of cash payments have led to widespread donor support and significantly increased funding for cash transfer programs[7] and the growth of effective organizations like GiveDirectly. Studies in rural Kenya have shown that basic income not only positively impacts individual households (which invest in things like livestock and better housing) but also benefits those in nearby villages and provides a stimulus for local economies. This evidence has disproven negative donor assumptions and prejudices and built support for not just GiveDirectly but the whole model of direct cash payments to reduce poverty.[8]

3. Mobilizing Others

In addition to helping you raise resources, robust evidence of impact allows you to amplify your influence, accelerating progress in achieving your mission. It helps you mobilize others in support of your cause. Evidence of impact can generate media interest. For example, stories about Give-Directly's impact have appeared in the *Economist* and other major publications and generated additional support for its mission and work.

Evidence of impact carries more weight with policymakers because they are often inured to inflated and unverified claims of nonprofit impact. And it can aid the work of peer organizations—particularly those who cannot afford to invest in robust impact measurement—as they can utilize your findings in their own programs and communications. Perhaps most critically, evidence can unlock more sustainable sources of funding and uptake by governments. In the case of cash transfers, long-term investment in evidence eventually convinced governments to begin using cash transfers as a form of poverty alleviation, with governments like Pakistan[9] and India[10] now distributing hundreds of millions in cash transfers to their populations.[11]

Another example comes from the organization More in Common, mentioned earlier. It works on a wide range of programs to reduce community polarization and the threat of "us-versus-them" divisions. For several years, they have advocated Canada's model of community-based refugee sponsorship as a policy that both inspires greater public confidence and results in better outcomes than traditional top-down refugee resettlement. More in Common conducts extensive polling of public perceptions, and they have consistently found that significantly higher numbers of Americans and Europeans will support the intake of refugees when they are directly sponsored by local communities. This evidence has been used widely by networks of refugee advocate policymakers and elected officials and has been highly influential with the US and UK governments in particular.*

---

* Notably, when Russia's invasion of Ukraine resulted in millions of Ukrainians fleeing for their lives, the US and UK established community-based schemes that mobilized hundreds of thousands of ordinary citizens as hosts and sponsors. Subsequent research on the experiences of hosts and sponsors also helped influence decisions in both countries to extend these schemes, such as through the Welcome

4. Accountability to Those You Serve and Your Staff

Properly measuring and communicating impact also allows your organization to build accountability and trust with the individuals and communities your organization serves, and provides them with evidence that you're upholding your commitments. It's not just donors who care about how charitable funds are spent. Those you serve also care deeply. If you want community members to actively participate in your work and give feedback, you need to show them you're holding up your end of the agreement. Providing concrete evidence of impact is also helpful if you work in an environment where, for whatever reason, people tend to be skeptical of civil society groups. The same goes for staff. Effective measurement of impact gives your staff a clear understanding of the change that their work is contributing to and can be a powerful motivating force.

THE CHALLENGES OF MEASURING IMPACT

When it comes to measuring impact, nonprofits commonly make four errors.

1. They measure overhead, not outcomes;
2. They measure what's easy, not what counts;

Corps initiative that US Secretary of State Anthony Blinken announced in January 2023. More in Common's strategy of providing robust quantitative and qualitative evidence of public attitudes shows that even on highly contested issues, there are pathways to influencing policymakers when you speak to their priorities (in this case, managing public opinion on a very sensitive issue). Matthew La Corte, L. J. Wolfgang Keppley, "New Poll Reveals Refugee Sponsorship Increases Support, Reduces Opposition to Resettlement," Niskanen Center website, March 1, 2021, https://www.niskanencenter.org/new-poll-reveals-refugee-sponsorship-increases-support-reduces-opposition-to-resettlement/; "Welcoming Ukrainians: The Hosts' Perspective," More in Common website, March 13, 2023, https://www.moreincommon.org.uk/our-work/research/welcoming-ukrainians/.

3. They decide that it is "impossible" to measure impact, so they don't try, instead of trying to find suitable proxies; and

4. They fail to distinguish between when they are having direct impact and when their impact is indirect (for example, by influencing systems).

We'll explore each in turn.

1. Overhead Is Not Impact

Given the challenges of assessing nonprofit performance, those seeking to do so (most often, donors) often turn to one thing they can measure easily—overhead. But overhead is an input. It is an organization's administrative and fundraising costs as a percentage of total expenditure. Some arbitrary overhead percentage (10 or 15 percent) is often set as a target. These costs are easy to measure, as they will be broken out in the organization's budget, but they tell you nothing about the organization's impact.

Overheads are a necessary cost of running a nonprofit. If you want to raise funds, you need to spend money on fundraising. If you want high-quality staff to carry out your ambitious mission, you need to invest in recruitment and training and benefits. If you want to run a tight financial ship, you need a strong finance team and good financial systems. All of these costs are overhead. Of course, it's always appropriate to ask whether or not you are spending the right amount on administration and fundraising, but that is about good management, not impact.

The superficial attraction of using overhead as a proxy for impact is the assumption that an organization with lower overhead is more efficient than a peer organization with larger costs. But this is not necessarily the case, as overhead is only relevant to the extent it drives impact or diverts resources from it. Nonprofits that invest more in their staff and internal systems will have higher overhead, but that may translate into greater impact than a peer that spends less on staff and internal systems.

It may also reduce the risks of something going wrong, such as financial malfeasance.* Those who judge organizations primarily by their overhead lack a fundamental understanding of how nonprofits work, and they overlook many high-performing organizations in the process.†

Business practice can provide a useful counterpoint. Because they have a clear metric to measure performance—namely, financial returns—no one seeks to compare businesses primarily on their overheads. Investors in Amazon or Tesla are not spending a lot of time comparing those organizations on the basis of what they spend on their sales, finance, or human resources departments. Rather, they're focused on their financial returns (impact) and factors that most directly impact those returns over time. Nonprofits should be judged similarly.

2. Measure What Matters

Inputs and activities are much easier to quantify than the results of those activities. But as has been wisely observed elsewhere: "Not everything that counts can be counted, and not everything that can be counted counts."[12]

Let's focus on the second half of that statement. As we saw in the previous section, overhead is often used as a measure of impact, as it's easy to measure, even though it doesn't tell you much about impact. The same often goes for activities. In this section we'll look at how the Freedom Fund moved from measuring what was easiest to count, to measuring

---

* Of course, there will also be organizations that are profligate with their spending and should be judged accordingly—but simply looking at a single overhead number won't tell you if that's the case. Rather, this requires a more detailed examination of the reasonableness of expenditure, particularly on fundraising. See Phil Buchanan, "Getting the Facts Straight About the Nonprofit Sector," *HuffPost*, September 23, 2013, www.huffpost.com/entry/getting-the-facts-straight_b_3976022/amp.

† For a vehement argument on the dangers of an undue focus on overhead, see Dan Pallotta, *Uncharitable: How Restraints on Nonprofits Undermine Their Potential* (Boston: Tufts University Press, 2010).

what really mattered. And then we'll look at the different situations that think tanks and advocacy organizations find themselves in as they try to measure their impact.

As I set out in the introduction to this chapter, at the Freedom Fund we started measuring direct impact in the form of "lives liberated" (as this was easier to count) and only later added other, more indirect, measures of impact, such as measurable reductions in slavery at the community level and at a broader systems level. This was our effort to measure what counts (i.e., overall reductions in the level of slavery).

The sustainability of your impact also counts. While the number of people in situations of trafficking (or poverty, hunger, etc.) in a community may decrease over the life span of a two-year program, will the rates go back up after the program is over, or after a few years? Are the interventions taking aim at alleviating the symptoms of a problem, or actually getting at root causes? If long-term sustainability is a part of your impact targets—that is, you aim to actually make a permanent or at least long-term impact on a person, community, or issue—then simply measuring impact at the end of a short-term program won't give you a good sense of whether those changes will stick.

These examples show us that the most obvious, direct output figures often don't tell the whole story, or even the right one. One way to improve impact measurement when it comes to modern slavery (or poverty, or hunger, or other societal change) is to focus on prevalence, i.e., the percentage of the population affected by the issue you are seeking to address. If we can start by establishing a baseline prevalence rate in a particular area before we start a program, then (ideally) we should be able to compare that to prevalence three, five, or ten years later to understand change over time. Using this approach, the Freedom Fund has been able to build a robust body of evidence, most of it generated through evaluations by leading research institutions, that shows that our approach has resulted in dramatic reductions in the prevalence of modern slavery in targeted communities over four-year periods.[13]

The second step to measuring prevalence reduction is assessing attribution. For example, modern slavery is tied to complex economic, social, and political systems and trends, so we can't automatically assume that our programs have caused a documented fall in rates of modern slavery; there could be other causes. For instance, if at the same time we were working with a community, the police (independently of our collective efforts) launched a sustained crackdown on traffickers, that would likely cause slavery numbers to fall significantly, and the change couldn't be attributed to our programs.

One way to assess attribution is to have a "control group," which in the Freedom Fund's case would be a group of vulnerable community members not being served by our programs, but similar in all other respects to the community being served. If the situation of the group being served improved more than the control group, that would be a strong indicator of the positive impact of the program.*

Rigorous prevalence studies are expensive and time-consuming, so we also measure activities that are strongly tied to a reduction in vulnerability to modern slavery—e.g., the number of at-risk children helped to return to school, the number of people provided with access to social and legal services, the number of micro-enterprises started, and the number of legal cases supported. More broadly, we also look at overall lives impacted by Freedom Fund–supported programs to understand our reach in comparison to funds spent.

The Freedom Fund's method of measuring impact is appropriate for our size, approach, and resources, but it won't be a fit for every

---

* A big challenge with control groups is that this kind of research can be very expensive. As an alternative, the Freedom Fund has in the past used participatory evaluations to try and "ground-truth" the results of our research—asking individual community members what they've seen and experienced to better understand the factors that led to a change in conditions. When we do this, we are always careful with our analysis, making sure not to overstate the role of our organization beyond what the data tells us.

organization or issue area. We have found success in tracking both outputs and outcomes over time. We've found that different audiences tend to seize on specific indicators that they deem important, and it has taken some effort to educate donors about why effective prevention efforts should eventually result in lower numbers of people liberated from slavery (because there will be fewer people left to liberate). But with a range of metrics that indicate lower levels of vulnerability to exploitation, complemented by long-term prevalence data, we are able to paint a much richer and more complex picture of the Freedom Fund's impact.

Think tanks face a very different challenge. Their difficulty in measuring impact often leads them to measure what they can count, not what matters. Think tanks will invariably count how many reports or opinion pieces they have published, or how many conferences they have convened. They may track how often their experts appear in the media, and how much traffic their website receives. These are all straightforward to count. And they are certainly a way to track productivity and profile. But they don't really capture impact.

This is because think tanks rarely see their primary purpose as publishing reports. Rather, their purpose is usually defined as generating ideas and evidence and influencing policymakers. As Ken Roth, the former CEO of global human rights organization Human Rights Watch, put it, his priority was "[e]nsuring that our programmatic work is always impact-oriented—that publications are not ends in themselves but tools to change governmental behavior."[14]

Counting reports or conferences won't tell you that. It won't tell you if those reports informed policy change or if they were even read. Measuring influence can be particularly challenging for think tanks and advocacy organizations because there are no direct measures. Policymakers rarely come out and say, "We took X action because we were persuaded by Y's report." However, that is not a reason for not trying to measure impact. In these cases, the best way to measure is via proxies for influence.

3. When You Can't Measure Directly, Find Proxies

When it is not possible or feasible to measure the impact of your work directly, then you must find proxies that give some clarity, and measure those rigorously, tracking your trajectory.[15] Perhaps the change you are looking to make is quite broad, and you need to find a specific metric that can be tracked relatively easily. For example, many international public health organizations looking to measure a community's access to healthcare use the percentage of children who have received the third dose of the diphtheria, tetanus, and pertussis vaccine as a proxy. These organizations figured out that since the vaccine requires three doses and therefore three separate interactions with the healthcare system over time, the third dose serves as a fairly accurate indicator of how strong and accessible the system is.[16] In some low-income countries, especially when economic data is sparse, nonprofits use the replacement of thatched roofs with more expensive corrugated metal ones as a proxy for poverty reduction.

CASE STUDY

How to Measure the Impact of a Think Tank

Faced with an economic recession, Arthur C. Brooks, the new president of the American Enterprise Institute (AEI), a free-markets think tank in Washington, DC, was under pressure to articulate the organization's impact more convincingly. But since much of what think tanks do is indirectly influence policy, a clear link between AEI's reports and its intended target, the thoughts and actions of American leaders, was hard to identify. Traditional evaluations like public opinion polls or legislative votes were not helpful in evaluating how demand for AEI's ideas measured up with those of other organizations. So Brooks turned to a set of proxy metrics that, when combined, allowed AEI to assess how well their ideas were being taken up. Over time, they tracked metrics like how many op-eds they landed in the most competitive media outlets (such as the *New York Times*, the *Wall Street Journal*, and the *Washington Post*) and how often they were invited to participate in congressional testimonies as compared to other think tanks. Each of these proxies was of limited use on its own but, when combined, Brooks could argue that AEI was living up to its definition of success: the influence and uptake of the ideas it generated. These metrics weren't only helpful for persuading donors; they also helped AEI leadership better assess how its programs were contributing to its ultimate goal.[17]

---

4. Indirect Impact and Systems Change

Organizations that aim to tackle thorny, deep-rooted social issues like poverty, gender inequality, and violence know that change doesn't happen through one type of intervention; many contributory factors need to be addressed. You don't sustainably reduce domestic violence just by providing shelter for victims or tackle poverty simply by providing cash handouts, even though these may be important interventions as part of a package of measures. Many factors are at play in these situations, and sustainable change requires addressing a number of them at the same time.

Complex systems—be they economic, political, social, or some combination of the three—call for complex solutions. As this understanding has taken hold in the nonprofit sector, the term "systems change" has emerged as a buzz-phrase. Though definitions can vary widely (Does it mean addressing root causes? Adapting to complexity? Bringing in "social entrepreneurs" who catalyze change across sectors?[18]), those of us focused on systems change can all agree that it is difficult to achieve and equally difficult to measure. If we are seeking to address these complex systems, we have to find ways to measure how our efforts and resources contribute to overall change, despite the challenges. This will often start with mapping out the various actors and issues that contribute to the problem, working out which of those actors and issues you can influence, and estimating how that might impact the system as a whole. As noted, none of this is easy, but if you don't try then everyone invested in your work is being asked to take it on trust that you are making a difference.

CASE STUDY

Measuring Changes to Communities' Vulnerability to Slavery

At the Freedom Fund, our work initially focused on direct support to those in slavery or at high risk of it. It was relatively straightforward to measure this impact in terms of individuals receiving services (such as victims liberated, individuals accessing social and legal services, at-risk children in school). But we soon became more ambitious and began to explore how our programs could address the systems that led to, and kept people in, slavery. The priority was not just getting individuals out of places where they were already being exploited but ensuring that those at risk didn't end up in slavery in the first place. This meant making sure that laws were properly enforced and government officials did their jobs (instead of turning a blind eye to exploitation); it meant helping vulnerable individuals get access to government benefits and subsidies they were entitled to, so they didn't get pushed into economic desperation; it meant changing norms, for example, by running information campaigns so people didn't just assume this was always the way things were done, and that nothing could or should change.

Our partners were engaging with governments and businesses, helping strengthen local social protection systems and running social and behavioral change campaigns. They were having striking success with these joined-up efforts, and we recognized this would have long-term, sustained impact far beyond the life cycle of our programs. When a law is changed, a legal precedent is set, or a business changes its sourcing practices, the effects are felt by populations far larger than those with whom our partners directly interact. But our impact measurement framework was set up to collect direct impact figures (e.g., numbers of individuals reached by specific services, numbers of people sustainably liberated from modern slavery), and other key proxies (e.g., numbers of media stories, prosecutions, and children returned to school). We had no way of counting the impact on those we couldn't see. We weren't measuring our impact on the system.

So we turned to our research team and gave them a challenge: experiment with a framework for measuring "indirect impact." (We define "indirect impact" as "beneficiaries who do not come into immediate contact with our grassroots partners and program activities, but nevertheless gain from the systems change that our program has contributed towards."[19]) We also set a new organizational target of reaching ten million individuals by 2025 by focusing on and measuring our contribution to systems change. This target was driven partly by interest from our board, as well as an observation of the great potential for systems-level shifts in our program areas and our desire to capture it.

Our team began by analyzing various forms of systems change and coming up with a three-level system of

categorization: protective environment, resilient communities, and empowered movement. Each of these categories describes a different level of impact, ranging from the
broadest population affected by changes like national legislation and public attitudes ("protective environment") down
to the more micro shifts experienced by stronger effectiveness and collaboration between anti-slavery leaders and
organizations ("empowered movement"). For each change
that we have either observed or are seeking to achieve in
our programs, we place it in one of these three categories
and, using available data, estimate the size of the population that would benefit. By the end of 2022, we estimated
we had indirectly impacted over seven million people.

We've added guardrails to avoid overcounting, keeping
estimates conservative and accounting for variance in the
status of implementation. This model of measurement is
far from perfect, and would be very expensive to validate
externally, but it has allowed us to find a way to evaluate
our contributions to systems change and to compare the
potential impact of various activities. In our experience, the
ability to experiment with new forms of impact measurement has been extremely valuable, leading us to new ways
to talk about our work and new strategic insights.

WHAT IF MEASURING IMPACT IS JUST TOO HARD?

It can be challenging for nonprofit leaders juggling limited resources,
multiple demands, and an ambitious mission to find the resources necessary to measure impact robustly. You might feel frustrated when told
what you should be measuring (by this book, or by multiple journal

articles), with the implication you are failing if your impact measurement isn't best-in-class.

The key takeaway should not be that you are failing unless you are conducting randomized control studies, baseline and endpoint prevalence surveys, or using sophisticated proxies. The most important thing to remember is that knowing what impact your efforts are having (or not) will help you ensure that your organization's actions align with its purpose. Investing time and thought into how your organization can improve is invariably a worthwhile investment, and one that will look different for everyone.

Regardless of where you are on this journey, take a hard look at how your organization understands its own impact. Then ask yourself if that process could be improved. It usually makes sense to measure your activities as part of your efforts to track impact. You can start by embedding basic systems of measurement within how you design, carry out, and evaluate a program. That way, you aren't left scrambling to track your impact retroactively. It particularly helps to measure your trajectory over time, as that can be a proxy for performance. Also, look at whether you can improve data collection. Can you better define the things you are measuring? Are there other particulars you can measure that will give a rounder picture of your work? Ask others for their input, particularly those you serve, and don't just ask your fans for input, but also those who are more skeptical of your work. How do peer organizations approach this?

———

All nonprofit leaders should strive to ensure their organizations have the greatest impact, whatever that may look like, using the resources available. A mindset focused on impact and better (if not perfect) ways of measuring it is the first step to achieving maximum impact. This mindset is also key to developing a powerful strategy, which is what we will look at in the next chapter.

IMPACT ACTION POINTS

Identify and Measure Change

- Work out the key inputs and activities of your nonprofit.
- Then identify the change (outcomes) your organization is seeking to bring about or contribute to.
- Assess how your organization is measuring its contribution to that change.
- Determine whether the measures being used can be sharpened, clarified, or expanded.
- If you can't rigorously measure your organization's impact, then explore whether you can improve the way you measure your activities and consider whether there are suitable proxies for impact that you can measure.
- Ensure you are making the best use of all the information your organization is generating.
- Regularly review and refine these efforts.

CHAPTER 3

Strategy

Make Choices to Maximize Impact

> [Strategy] is the alignment of potentially unlimited aspira-
> tions with necessarily limited capabilities.
>
> —John Lewis Gaddis[1]

W endy Kopp was a final-year undergraduate student at Princeton University, with a deep interest in education reform,
when she came up with the bold idea that was to shape the
rest of her professional career and shake up the education sector in the US
and beyond. The problem she wanted to address was the desperate shortage of qualified teachers for the lowest-income communities throughout
the country.* She outlined her proposed strategy in her senior thesis:

---

* The lack of support for these communities has significant longer-term consequences. An influential report in 1999 highlighted the resulting "achievement gap":
"By the time they are nine years old, students in low-income areas will already be
three to four grade levels behind nine-year olds in high-income areas . . . And with
such extreme disparities that start at such an early age, it should be of no surprise,
that children from low-income families are seven times less likely than children

Why not get the country's best minds to commit two years to teach in urban and rural public schools? It would change the lives of some of the nation's most underserved students, and it would change the consciousness and direction of our nation's future leaders.[2]

Of course, getting the "best minds" (i.e., graduates from some of the top universities) to commit to two years of teaching was easier said than done, given all the other options open to them. But this is where Wendy leaned into the purpose of her initiative. What she could offer to graduates that corporate recruiters couldn't was a compelling cause. As she put it: "I had this sense that there were thousands of people out there—talented, driven people—who were not inspired by the opportunities they saw in front of them, who were searching for something they weren't finding in terms of the opportunity to assume a significant responsibility that would make a real difference."[3]

Wendy didn't just rely on the power of her cause. She made the recruitment process for her new teacher corps—by now called Teach For America—highly selective, in order to make it more attractive to overachieving graduates. She went around to leading universities, such as Harvard, Yale, and Princeton, with the message, "If you're really good, you might be able to join our cause. But first you have to submit to a rigorous screening and evaluation process. You should prepare yourself for rejection because it takes a special capability to succeed in these classrooms."[4] And if they succeeded in getting selected, their reward was to work with students who have been badly served by the education sector in the past, in low-income communities, at the same entry-level pay as other new teachers in the state.

---

from high-income families to graduate from college." Patte Barth, Jeanne Brennan, Kati Haycock, Karen Mora, and others, "Education Watch 1998," *The Education Trust State and National Data Book*, Vol. 2, 1999, 1–24, cited in Sarah Thorp (2000), Teach For America, HBS 9-300-084, hbsp.harvard.edu/cases/.

Of course, recruiting talented graduates was just one part of the challenge. The other was raising funding for an innovative and wholly untested educational start-up. Wendy and her small team worked around the clock, relentlessly pitching corporations and foundations for funding, selling them on the idea of transforming education for the most underserved in the country while giving a sense of purpose to high-performing graduates. It worked. By the end of its first year, Teach For America had recruited five hundred graduates for its inaugural cohort of teachers.

Over the next five years, Teach For America grew rapidly. It expanded its remit beyond its own teacher recruitment and placement efforts to reforming school programs and providing recruiting services on a contract basis to school districts. In fact, it grew so quickly that by its fifth year it found its ambitions were exceeding the funding it could mobilize. As a result, it had to make some painful course corrections. This included reducing its annual expenditure from $8 million to $5 million, achieved in part by letting go sixty experienced teachers who provided professional development to the newer teachers. It also closed down its contract recruiting services initiative and some other, non-core, projects. These were deeply painful cuts for a young and ambitious organization, but they ensured that Teach For America could remain focused on its core mission of getting young graduates to work with low-income students.[5] This discipline set it up for long-term success.

Some thirty years later, Teach For America has approximately 64,000 alumni. Of those, 1,300 are currently principals, assistant principals, and deans, and more than 14,800 are teachers. Its alumni have taught millions of students in the US. Its recruitment focus and corps makeup have evolved to become more representative of the students its serves—now half of its corps members identify as people of color, half come from a low-income background, and one-third are first-generation college graduates.[6] Statewide studies of the relative effectiveness of teacher education programs consistently place Teach For America at or near the top in terms of participants' effects on student academic outcomes.[7]

Its impact is not limited to the US. Teach For America–affiliated organizations have now been set up in sixty-one countries, ranging from Peru to Pakistan, dramatically increasing the reach of the organization's purpose and mission. But at its heart remains Wendy's original idea—to persuade top graduates to devote two years of their life to serving students in the lowest-income communities.*

I started this chapter with Teach For America's origin story because I've always found it to be an inspiring example of strategy in action. Strategy for a nonprofit is the set of decisions and trade-offs it needs to make to achieve the greatest impact.† In this case, Wendy identified a clearly defined problem and found an innovative way to mobilize the necessary resources by leaning into the intrinsic motivation of a powerful cause. Her great insight was to turn the challenge of recruiting top talent on its head—by challenging bright graduates to prove they had what it takes to make a difference to the lives of those who could most benefit from top-quality education. Relentless execution and a willingness to make tough choices when the organization began drifting off mission have all contributed to the outsized impact Teach For America has had on the education sector.

---

* The global umbrella organization is Teach For All. For more on Teach For All, listen to the Wendy Kopp interview on the *System Catalysts* podcast, "Creating an Education Leadership Movement with Teach For All."

† Some other definitions of nonprofit strategy: "A planned set of actions that are designed to achieve its mission," Meehan and Jonker, *Engine of Impact*, 46. "Getting critical resource decisions right—allocating time, talent, and dollars to the activities that have the greatest impact—is what 'strategy' is all about," Susan Colby, Nan Stone, and Paul Carttar, "Zeroing In on Impact," *Stanford Social Innovation Review*, Fall 2004. One of the leading academics on corporate strategy, Michael Porter, describes it as "deliberately choosing a different set of activities to deliver a unique mix of value," Michael E. Porter, "What Is Strategy," *Harvard Business Review*, November/December 1996.

WHAT IS STRATEGY?

Every nonprofit has a strategy. It may be written or unwritten. A strategy provides a conceptual framework for the most effective allocation of your organization's resources (people, money, and time). A good strategy enables you to make the best decisions for your organization in the circumstances you face, to achieve the greatest impact. A bad strategy may be the decision to continue spending money to implement existing programs, despite evidence showing they are having little impact.

So, what does strategy look like when done *well*? There is no universal template, but I'll set out a few key concepts and approaches that I think are of value, based on my firsthand experience with a number of strategic planning processes. My hope is that these will help guide you as you decide on the approach that best works for your organization.

The objective should always be to end up with a clear plan or framework that guides your organization's work and that you can revise as circumstances require. So how to do that?

1. The starting place is to embark on a thoughtful **strategic planning process**. Good planning is key, and an essential first step in designing a strategy. In fact, to my mind, the planning process is often more valuable than any written strategic plan that results.

2. The next step is to ensure you have a powerful **mission** in place, or develop one as part of the planning process. As discussed in chapter one, that means being clear about your organization's purpose and how you intend to achieve it.

3. You should have an idea of the impact you hope to achieve in the next few years—your **impact goals**—as this provides a way of assessing your progress and gives your organization something to aim for. In a start-up, these goals may be based more on guesswork than evidence, but you should still have some idea of what you hope to achieve. Once your organization is more established, you should aim to have more specific targets for

your impact within a clear time frame—usually three to five years, though sometimes longer. In setting these targets, you will remain guided by your mission, as they will help you gauge whether you are on track to deliver on that mission.

4.   You need a clear understanding of the path to achieve your mission and impact goals. This means analyzing how your organization's activities (and its programs in particular) will translate into impact, directly or indirectly, and defining the key assumptions you are making in the process. This analysis is usually called your "**theory of change**."*

5.   As you are deciding what you will set out to do, you also have to decide what you *won't* do. That means making choices! This can be challenging, particularly if it means closing underperforming programs or reallocating resources.

6.   Once all of this is clear, you can set out your strategy as a written plan or framework, bearing in mind that even the most thoughtful plan will likely need to change and adapt over time.

We'll look at each of these steps in turn, but first I'll share some of the initial strategic decisions I had to make when the Freedom Fund launched.

CASE STUDY

Making Early Strategic Choices at the Freedom Fund

The importance of making choices and trade-offs was starkly brought home to me in my first couple of months as CEO of the Freedom Fund. This was because I had to make a number of important decisions very early on, which I knew

---

* This is sometimes also written in the format of a "log frame," or logical framework. I'll stick with "theory of change" here.

would have lasting implications for the organization—even though we were still very much in a setup phase. Bear in mind that, at this stage, we had a team of three. We were yet to find our own offices and were camping out in the building of a friendly think tank. We were still sorting out some of the basics, such as our charitable registration and payroll and insurance. But our board had made clear that it expected us to achieve significant impact in our first five years—on the lives of hundreds of thousands of highly vulnerable people—even while knowing that a long lead time was required to properly set up anti-slavery programs and build the partnerships and trust needed to make lasting changes.

The board's directive meant we had to start quickly, making some big decisions on how we would operate, even though I knew we didn't have all the information I would have liked at that stage. We had to work out how to get operational quickly, while we were still staffing up. We had to balance the urgency to launch programs, with the risks inherent in running programs in countries with a high burden of slavery. Despite everything that still needed to be done in the short term, we already needed to be looking forward four or five years to envision how we would like the organization to be placed then if everything came together as planned. And we had to ensure we had the ability to quickly change course if it became apparent that we had got any of the big calls wrong.

Given all of that, in consultation with my small team and our board members, we decided:

1. Instead of concentrating all our initial programs in India, home to the highest number of people in slavery, we would spread the programs between South Asia, Southeast Asia, and Africa to provide greater diversity in geography and types of exploitation to be addressed. This

also ensured that we did not have all our programmatic "eggs" in one country's "basket." While we recognized that we could achieve considerable impact by focusing all our resources on a single country with a particularly high burden of slavery, we believed that starting with a more diverse set of programs and countries would be of broader use to the anti-slavery field, appeal to a greater range of potential funders, and reduce the risks inherent in being limited to a single country.*

2. Instead of implementing the initial programs ourselves, taking the time to recruit and build our program team from scratch, we engaged (and paid) a trusted partner organization with on-the-ground expertise and teams already in place to implement them according to our directions. This would allow us to get programs up and running much more rapidly (which was essential if we were to meet ambitious impact goals). This also gave us the time to build up our own team while still maintaining ownership of program design and research.

3. We spent precious funding reserves on high-quality research from the start, instead of waiting until we had raised dedicated funding for research. For example, we commissioned baseline surveys as soon as our programs launched so that in a few years' time we would be well placed to measure the change to which our programs had contributed. This was a significant up-front

---

* This proved to be a wise decision when the Indian government in 2021 stopped us from funding frontline partners in that country—causing us to close down our work there in 2023. What could have been a huge blow for the organization if we had concentrated the bulk of our programs in that high-prevalence country was cushioned by the fact that we were already operational in a number of other countries by then.

investment for returns that would only eventuate in a few years, but, given that the Freedom Fund's mission included addressing the deficit of credible research, we decided it was one worth prioritizing.

In hindsight, these turned out to be the right decisions to best position the organization to achieve high impact in the years ahead. We got a number of programs up and running in our first eighteen months, much earlier than if we had first waited to build our own teams. When we embarked on a more formal strategic planning process three years later, we doubled down on geographic diversity and investment in research, but we also decided that the time was right to bring implementation of our programs in-house as we now had the team in place to do that well and a strong desire to have more control over our programs.

PLANNING IS OFTEN MORE IMPORTANT THAN THE PLAN ITSELF

The planning process is where you consider a range of scenarios and responses and start making choices. It's where you align your organization's big aspirations with its necessarily limited capabilities. As such, it can be invaluable. Former US president Dwight D. Eisenhower put it this way: "Plans are worthless, but planning is everything."[8] In other words, the environments we operate in are full of uncertainty and unknowns— or, as former US world heavyweight boxer Mike Tyson put it, "Everybody has a plan until they get punched in the mouth." That being the case, a detailed written plan based on a single scenario will likely prove inadequate to guide decisions over any period of time. But if you're willing to commit the time and energy, the process of coming up with your plan can be highly insightful and informative for your future strategy.

Picture a nonprofit working on mental health and loneliness in March 2020, largely dependent on fundraising from individual and corporate donors. Now imagine this organization had recently finalized a detailed five-year strategic plan running from January 2020 to December 2024, projecting a steady expansion of income and services based on its progress over the last five years and assuming a stable economic environment. Three months into the strategy, an unexpected and unprecedented global pandemic leads to the closure of workplaces and schools around the world. This in turn fuels an explosion in demand for this nonprofit's services, at the same time driving a significant drop in income as donors retreat in the face of great economic uncertainty. The strategy would go out the window.*

You might respond that COVID-19 was a once-in-a-generation event, and hopefully you are right. But so are the economic crises driven by the war in Ukraine and its fallout at a time of global fragility, or the long overdue racial justice reckoning following the murders of George Floyd, Ahmaud Arbery, Breonna Taylor, and too many others—all of which can and should have big implications for nonprofit strategies. What can be planned for, or at least explored, are things like big swings in income or demand, or sudden changes in government policy or the political climate.

Good planning requires you to consider various scenarios and give thought to how you will respond. You can seek to put all of this in a written plan, though the more detailed it is, the sooner it is likely to become irrelevant. Rather, you should state what you want to achieve by when, broadly describe how you think you can best achieve that, with underlying assumptions, and be willing to constantly review and adjust your strategy as circumstances change.

---

* I talk more about how the COVID pandemic had an impact on the Freedom Fund, and forced us to rapidly change our strategy, in the chapter on People.

One nonprofit governance expert likens this to the contrast between the era of using paper maps to navigate while driving and the current era, where GPS systems and smartphones (satellite navigation, or "satnav") are most commonly used:

> The "Maps" world consisted of incredibly detailed and lengthy strategic plans and annual budgets. The "Satnav" world . . . consists of strategic frameworks and parameters and dynamic budgeting. I.e., making decisions, at the best time, with the very latest information.[9]

In this example, we need to move from creating static "maps" and toward dynamic plans that allow us to adjust our actions based on changing contexts. But this presupposes that you do your planning well. Sadly, bad planning is all too common. This is not surprising, given that nonprofits have the difficult-to-define objective of delivering the greatest possible impact. They also have multiple stakeholders (e.g., staff, communities served, donors, board, partners) with a vested interest in the strategy and power to influence its formulation, which can result in a protracted and sometimes problematic process when formulating strategy. As a consequence, too many nonprofits engage in drawn-out, unfocused, and expensive planning processes, which result in less-than-ideal strategies. But it doesn't have to be this way. A successful planning process requires a number of things:

1. The roles of those participating in the process need to be clearly delineated. Staff absolutely should be involved, and consulted, but the strategy shouldn't be drafted by a committee of the whole organization. The same goes for other key partners and constituencies, such as your funders and, particularly, those your organization serves. You also need to engage closely with your board members, as they will ultimately sign off on the strategy, so the more they engage with the key issues being

considered, the more likely they will be to support the strategy that results.

2. Clarity around key questions is vital. For example: Is your mission (still) fit for purpose? What kind of impact are you seeking to achieve, over what time frame, and with what resources? What funding is out there for your cause? How will your programs deliver the impact you are aiming for? What scenarios may impact your ability to deliver? What are peer organizations doing? Clarity on these matters will also support more effective consultation, and hence better decision-making.

3. When circumstances change (e.g., pandemic or economic crisis), or things don't develop as planned (e.g., hoped-for funding doesn't come through, or activities don't translate into impact as expected), there must be a willingness to make difficult choices, such as what to stop doing, or not do in the first place, rather than ignoring or overlooking them.

Whatever your planning process, as part of that process you will need to review your mission, consider the impact that you wish to achieve in a defined time frame, and determine your theory of change. We'll look at each of these in turn.

REVIEW THE MISSION WHEN SETTING STRATEGY

It's often helpful to define or revise your mission at the same time you prepare your strategy, as the mission and impact go hand in hand. To decide what you are going to do and for whom, you need to spend time thinking about the impact you want to achieve, the various scenarios you may face, and how you can best deliver the change you seek to achieve. This all feeds into the process of defining your mission and setting your strategy. Returning to our example of the very well-funded shelter for the homeless in a gentrifying part of San Francisco,* if you were engaging in a new strategic planning process for that organization, now would be the time to revisit its mission and impact goals, and revise both of them in light of the fact that your nonprofit clearly has the opportunity and resources to be much more ambitious and hence have a greater impact in pursuit of its purpose.

IDENTIFY THE IMPACT YOU EXPECT TO HAVE OVER THE NEXT FEW YEARS

Given that your nonprofit exists to make a positive change in the world, to be effective you need to be able to set out what you are trying to achieve, and for whom, within a reasonable time frame. These are your impact goals, sometimes called intended impact. They can be general, particularly in the early days of the organization, or more specific when you have a better idea of what you can realistically achieve. Shaped by your mission, they are usually set for three to five years, as that's about as far out as most organizations can comfortably plan. But sometimes they are longer, and sometimes you might have a combination of both shorter- and longer-term goals.

These goals can reflect the impact that your organization can achieve directly or indirectly, on your own or in collaboration with others, as we explored in the previous chapter.

DETERMINE THE THEORY OF CHANGE

"Theory of change" is the most important component of strategy for nonprofits. It's the insight that powers your organization. It explains why the things your nonprofit is doing will produce the change you want to

---

* See chapter one, Mission.

see. If your organization doesn't have that insight, and act on it, it will struggle to succeed. And if the insight is wrong, then your organization may well fail to bring about the change it seeks to achieve.

A more technical description of theory of change is that it "explains how the organization's intended impact will actually happen, the cause-and-effect logic by which organizational and financial resources will be converted into the desired social results."*[10]

To return to our example of Teach For America, its theory of change in its formative years was that the organization would bring exceptional talent into education and then cultivate and develop that talent to create lifelong leaders working to drive change for low-income kids.[11]

Theory of change is important for nonprofits because their goals are usually ambitious, and difficult to measure accurately. Nonprofits are often operating in an environment where many others are seeking to achieve the same or similar impact, so attribution can be a challenge: If ten organizations are working to tackle child poverty in a particular city, how do you explain how your organization's work is making a difference? A good theory of change will explain why the specific activities of your organization are contributing to the change you seek to bring about. Because your assumptions are made explicit, those scrutinizing your work can better make their own assessment as to your contribution.

Take, for example, two nonprofits working to reduce levels of teen pregnancy in Arizona. One advocates sex education as the most effective method to do so. Its theory of change—its insight—is that

---

* Another useful explanation is: "A theory of change is the empirical basis underlying any social intervention—for example, the belief that a young person's close relationship with adult role models can reduce his susceptibility to violence, or that regular visits by registered nurses to first-time pregnant women can improve parenting skills and children's outcomes." Paul Brest, "The Power of Theories of Change," *Stanford Social Innovation Review*, Spring 2010.

better-informed youth make better choices about when and how to have sex, and it shapes its mission and programming accordingly. The other promotes teen abstinence as the best approach. Its theory of change is that only by encouraging teens to stop having sex can we reduce pregnancies. Now, assume during the last five years in which they have both been operating that there has been a significant reduction in teen pregnancy in Arizona. Which organization can claim credit for this—that is, which model is more effective? Absent expensive research studies on both organizations' work in the state, it will be difficult to answer this. But now assume there are robust studies in other US states showing that comprehensive sex education was far more effective than abstinence in reducing teen pregnancy levels there. (In fact, we can do more than assume—a large body of research shows that abstinence-only education is correlated with higher teenage pregnancy and birth rates.*) Even if this research is not explicitly focused on Arizona, it gives greater credibility to the theory of change of the sex education nonprofit than that of its abstinence-focused counterpart because there is evidence in support of its assumptions.

Nonprofit leaders need to spend time understanding theory of change, because it links the measurable work of nonprofits with their larger objectives, and hence provides a degree of rigor to the work. The reasoning behind theory of change is that when we look at the outcome we want to achieve, we can usually generate empirical data on our intermediate steps (our activities), even if we can't measure the

---

* See, for example, "Abstinence Education Programs: Definition, Funding, and Impact on Teen Sexual Behavior," Kaiser Family Foundation website, June 1, 2018, www.kff.org/womens-health-policy/fact-sheet/abstinence-education-programs -definition-funding-and-impact-on-teen-sexual-behavior/; and Kathrin F. Stanger-Hall and David W. Hall, "Abstinence-Only Education and Teen Pregnancy Rates: Why We Need Comprehensive Sex Education in the US," 2011, *PLoS ONE*, 6(10). https://doi.org/10.1371/journal.pone.0024658.

outcome itself in a robust way. So, think tanks can measure reports published, and number of meetings with policymakers, if not policy change directly resulting from their reports and advocacy. Or, while nonprofits may be able to measure outcomes, they can't always measure their contributions, not least when others have also contributed to those outcomes (such as in the teen pregnancy example earlier). Thus, we need a way to logically explain how our activities contributed or mobilized others to contribute.

A good theory of change is helpful as you develop your strategy because, as you make decisions or consider scenarios, you can use the framework of the theory to consider how these decisions and scenarios will likely contribute to (or detract from) impact goals. But, of course, your theory of change will only be as good as the quality of the data you have, and the quality of the insight underlying it (e.g., comprehensive sex education versus abstinence). Over time, ideally, you will accumulate more and more data to validate that your theory of change is fit for purpose. You will move from apparent effectiveness to demonstrated effectiveness, and from anecdotal findings to empirical evidence.

STRATEGY INVOLVES TRADE-OFFS

By definition, making a decision to follow a particular course of action also means making a decision not to pursue alternatives. Teach For America had to do this in its early years, closing down a couple of its initiatives—and its willingness to make tough choices set it up for longer-term success. Likewise, when the Freedom Fund got started, we had to choose between a set of alternatives, such as investing deeply in one country or more broadly in a range of countries. As you allocate your key resources of funding and staff, you must decide where they will have the greatest impact. This means choosing between a range of options. Doing this well is key to effective strategy.

That said, too often in the nonprofit world leaders seek to avoid tough decisions. Frequently, they are reluctant to decide between attractive options or stop doing something they have started, even if it's not having the intended impact. But if everything is a priority, nothing is. Businesses have their financial bottom line and relentless competitive pressure to help concentrate their minds on the need to make choices and trade-offs. That's often not the case for nonprofits and, lacking such discipline, they often pursue too many options. Or they put off necessary decisions, like closing a failing program or making cuts to staff or other expenditures in a fraught financial situation. But, of course, not deciding is a decision in itself—just not a very good one in most circumstances when action is required.

Robust planning, a clear understanding of your mission and the impact you want to achieve, and a thoughtful theory of change will all help you make the right decisions. And by making the right decisions and trade-offs, you'll be pursuing the most effective strategy for your organization and positioning it to make the greatest impact.

My experience in so many different contexts has always underscored for me that purpose shapes everything that nonprofits do in their efforts to drive change. The concept of purpose is both amorphous and empowering. It's amorphous because it can be difficult to translate into concrete results—namely, impact. This amorphousness is a key difference between nonprofits and businesses, as the latter have much clearer metrics by which to measure progress and success. That is why strategy is so important to nonprofits, as it sets the path by which they translate purpose into concrete results. But the concept is also empowering, because pursuing positive change is inherently motivating for staff, and gives leaders a superb tool to build a highly effective team, which is what we will explore in the next section on people.

STRATEGY ACTION POINTS

Make Choices to Maximize Impact

- Understand the importance of planning and the difference between planning and the resulting strategic plan.
- Review your organization's mission and make sure it is (still) fit for purpose.
- Seek to identify the impact you hope to have over the next three to five years (or another defined period). This is your organization's intended impact.
- Explain how your activities, and your programs in particular, will translate into the desired impact, and set this out in your theory of change.
- Internalize that you need to make choices about what your organization will and won't do, to ensure it has the maximum impact with the available resources.
- Set all of this out in your written strategic plan or framework, understanding that it will need to evolve as circumstances change.

PEOPLE

Build the Organization

No matter how brilliant your mind or strategy, if you're playing a solo game, you'll always lose out to a team.

—Reid Hoffman[1]

At the beginning of 2020, the Freedom Fund was in a good place. The organization was six years old and growing quickly in size, impact, and reputation. We had solid finances. Our staff surveys showed consistently high levels of staff satisfaction. We were in the first year of implementing a new strategic framework. We had plans to expand into a couple of new countries and deepen our work to build a movement of women and survivor leaders.

Then COVID-19 hit. Like everyone else that March, we could see it coming. We closed our biggest office, in London, a week before the UK government mandated it. We then rapidly shuttered the rest of our offices around the world. Soon after, distressing reports started coming in from our programs of the devastating toll that the disease and lockdowns were exacting on the highly vulnerable communities we worked with in Brazil, Ethiopia, India, Myanmar, Nepal, and Thailand. There was going to be a significant increase in exploitation of these communities—in the form of sex trafficking, forced labor, and child marriage—as desperate people took ever greater risks to survive, while being preyed upon by those all too willing to exploit desperation.

This perfect storm presented me with the most challenging situation I had ever confronted as a leader. I was desperately worried about the impact the pandemic would have on the vulnerable populations we served and our ability to support them in these hard times, especially if our own organization started struggling. I was deeply concerned about the health and safety of our staff, particularly those in low-income countries with overwhelmed health services. I was apprehensive that the stress of the pandemic might undermine staff motivation and cohesion. I was nervous about our finances; would the pandemic cause our donors to cut their funding, given the febrile economic climate? And, like most others, I found lockdown hugely challenging for my own well-being. In my case, my two daughters lived in Brussels with my ex-wife, normally a two-hour train ride away through the tunnel under the English Channel. I used to spend every second weekend with them, but restrictions on international travel meant I didn't get to meet up with them for the first three months of the pandemic, causing me considerable distress.

In the midst of all of this, I had to work out how to best lead the organization through this unprecedented crisis. I concluded early on that keeping our organization's purpose—to serve the most vulnerable—front and center in our response would be motivating and empowering for our staff in these uncertain times. We were all acutely conscious that vulnerable populations were going to be the hardest hit by this pandemic. Serving them gave us something to unify around. But this was easier said than done. How would a focus on purpose translate into concrete action?

I decided that the first order of business was to ensure stability within the organization at a time of great flux, so we were best placed to carry out our mission. Then we would double down on that mission.

To provide stability, I had to adapt my leadership style. In recent years I had worked to bring more of a coaching style to my leadership, focused on supporting staff to achieve their goals. This style was well suited to "peacetime" leadership. But this crisis required a more authoritative approach. I needed to project calm confidence and reassure staff that we were well placed to weather the crisis and support those we served, even if I wasn't entirely confident that that was the case.

As a first step, I convened an all-staff call in late March. I said we had the financial resources to weather the pandemic through the rest of the calendar year at the very least, and that we would not need to lay off any of our staff or make any cuts to salaries or funding to partner organizations. I believed that to be the case, but it would be dependent on our funders standing by us. My next step was to reach out to all of those funders, many represented on our board. To their credit, they all maintained their funding, and several increased it.

The next priority was our mission. To support the many frontline organizations we partnered with in low-income countries—who were buckling under the weight of pandemic-driven demand—we made our funding highly flexible so that they could determine their priorities in this time of crisis. Many of them used the funding for emergency food and medical supplies for local communities. We then went further and set up an emergency response fund for which we raised millions of dollars in additional funding from existing donors and some new ones. That fund not only had the very direct benefit of providing additional resources to frontline partners at a time of deep need but provided our funders and staff with a concrete way to respond to the crisis, giving them a sense of direction and agency at a time when many were overwhelmed by the suffering we were seeing in our program countries.

I was impressed, and moved, by how well our whole organization pulled together. It was a testament to the culture we had collectively built for the organization over the previous six years. Consistent with that culture, the leadership team was transparent with staff about the unfolding situation, the risks we faced, and our plans to mitigate them. In turn, we asked staff to be flexible and to recognize we were operating in unprecedented times, and that our primary responsibility was to provide even greater support to the communities we served.

The organization rapidly adjusted to remote working. Teams found different ways to communicate and share information even though they couldn't meet in person. Our approach of working closely with frontline organizations proved to be a particularly effective model during this time of crisis when many of the bigger, more centralized international nonprofit organizations were hamstrung by their unwieldy top-down model and overly dependent on expatriate leadership.

It was a difficult time. All of our staff in India had family members or friends who died of COVID-19, as did many other staff in countries such as Ethiopia and Brazil. The toll on vulnerable communities was appallingly high. But it would have been even higher if not for our ability to provide support throughout the pandemic.

We came out of those two years a stronger and more cohesive organization. By the time the worst of the pandemic was over in early 2022, staff morale was even higher than it had been before the pandemic started, according to our internal surveys. We had expanded our programs and had gained new funders, ending up in a more robust financial position than we started—all the better to meet the increased demand for our support following the pandemic.

I have a number of reflections as I look back on those early days of the pandemic, now that the worst appears well and truly behind us. The crisis powerfully reinforced my belief in the importance of effective leadership and culture and teams, and the motivational power of purpose. Culture was absolutely key. In times of crisis, what mattered most were the unwritten rules and behaviors of the organization as a whole, and of teams within the organization. These couldn't be created on the fly but needed months and years of investment. Our purpose was a constant throughout and helped all of us maintain a sense of direction and commitment. It underpinned our culture.

And that's what I want to talk about in this section. We will first look at the CEO, the most senior member of the organization's people. We will identify the issues a CEO should prioritize amid the multiple claims on their time and attention. We'll explore leadership styles, and how successful nonprofit leaders use purpose as a motivating force. We will then examine why creating a positive, purpose-focused culture is so important to the effective operation of the organization as a whole and teams within it. As organizations navigate a time of significant social ferment and change, we will explore the importance of embedding diversity, equity, and inclusion into an organization's values and culture and how, done well, this further strengthens the culture. Finally, we'll look at one particular category of your people, namely your board members, and the importance of maintaining a strong and productive relationship between the board and the CEO.

CHAPTER 4

The CEO

Determine Your Priorities and Style

> *Leadership is not defined by the exercise of power but by the capacity to increase the sense of power among those led. The most essential work of the leader is to create more leaders.*
>
> —Mary Parker Follett[1]

My most bruising, and formative, leadership experience involved a staff rebellion caused by my serious mishandling of events. It unfolded in the depths of the financial crisis in 2009. At the time I was deputy president of the International Crisis Group, with overall responsibility for our operations, finance, and human resources. Given the hugely uncertain financial environment, the board directed the organization to cut spending by 10 percent, which I fully agreed with. A few days later, senior staff left for a long-planned retreat in the medieval Belgian town of Bruges, a few hours from Crisis Group's headquarters in Brussels. It could have been a timely occasion for senior staff to thoughtfully work through the savings we would need to make. But that was not how I approached it.

77

From the first time I led a small team at work, I had always been a decisive leader. This style had served me well. I liked making decisions and enjoyed the responsibility. But I was not a consultative leader; I was more unilateral in my decision-making. I tended to see consultation and consensus-building as an unnecessary constraint on my decision-making power—as something that slowed a team down and obstructed timely action.

The CEO had given me broad responsibility to work out how best to make the savings, in a way that would have the minimum impact on the organization's overall effectiveness. My first priority was to make cuts as quickly as possible, so we would start benefiting from the savings immediately. And the second was to focus on making a few deep cuts—mainly to staff in lower-priority areas, or who were not performing well—rather than squeezing the entire organization. I thought that to achieve these outcomes, it would be better to barrel through quickly, rather than consult with all our senior staff and face coordinated pushback. Accordingly, in the short time between our board meeting and our retreat, I identified a number of staff members who would need to go, and a couple of other robust savings measures. I got the sign-off from the CEO and then advised relevant supervisors which of their staff were to be made redundant. That was the state of play when we all arrived in Bruges.

Not surprisingly, my decisions were not well received by senior staff, who objected to the lack of consultation and to many of the proposed measures. They responded by convening their own late-night meeting, excluding the CEO, finance director, and me. The next morning they demanded one of them chair the retreat in place of the CEO and insisted that we reopen the whole process and work together collectively to decide on the best course of action. This was a seismic development for an organization long accustomed to an authoritative, verging on authoritarian, CEO. That said, the CEO handled this all pretty graciously, given the direct challenge to his authority, perhaps sensing now was not the time to try to impose his will. For my part, I was deeply distressed at the way events were unfolding and the realization that my mishandling of the process had led to a staff revolt. But I also accepted that, having mismanaged the process, I now needed to swallow my pride and work with senior staff to come up with the best outcome.

A few things happened as we huddled in groups to explore program and department budgets across the organization. First, it became clear that senior staff members were not opposed to making savings. They all understood the imperative, but believed we could identify the right strategies better collectively than in isolation. The most senior layer of staff volunteered reductions in their salaries. Many of our program teams proposed savings that hadn't already been identified. Of course, this meant that we would end up squeezing the organization as a whole rather than identifying discrete areas for deep savings, but I'd surrendered that opportunity by making that decision on my own. On the plus side, this turn of events meant that all of our senior staff were brought into the decision-making process, and they committed to bringing the rest of our staff along with the need for savings.

Within a year of the retreat, we had reduced expenditure by 15 percent, and the following year we had secured enough new income to invest more heavily in priority areas. As for me, I learned two important things: First, that being "decisive" did not mean that I had to be unilateral in my decision-making or that I couldn't or shouldn't consult and engage others in decisions that directly affected them. And second, that a thoughtful process and consultation will generally lead to better outcomes with greater buy-in. I've taken this to heart ever since. Perhaps all of this should have been obvious from the beginning, but I suspect many new leaders worry that engaging others in their decision-making is a sign of weakness, rather than the demonstration of confidence that it should be. We all learn along the way. I certainly did.

HOW SHOULD YOU LEAD?

Stepping into the CEO role for the first time is daunting, whether at a start-up nonprofit or a big, well-established charity. The job becomes only marginally less daunting after you have been leading for a while. You are always hugely aware of all of the responsibility that comes with leadership: to inspire staff and other key stakeholders with your vision for the organization; raise enough funding to keep the doors open and, hopefully, grow; manage sometimes tricky board and staff dynamics; design and implement the strategy; and deliver impact. For me, the heaviest burden is the recognition that if I fail, those we serve—for the Freedom Fund, some of the world's most vulnerable people—will likely not get the support they desperately need, and staff may be out of a job. The buck always stops with the CEO.

So, let's assume you are a recently appointed CEO. You have a torrent of questions rushing through your mind about how to be the best leader you can be—and an overflowing inbox. In my experience, there are four aspects of leadership a leader needs to think through. These are: your priorities, your style, your own well-being, and (eventually) your successor. Let's take each of these in turn.

YOUR PRIORITIES

In recent years I've been coaching a number of nonprofit leaders in Africa, Europe, and the US, most of them new to the CEO role. A common challenge identified by nearly every CEO I coach is that they struggle to determine what they should prioritize, given the multiple pressing demands on their time. Being new to the role, they find that everyone wants a piece of them, resulting in them being pulled in too many directions. While they generally understand that if they try to do too many things they will likely do none of them well, it is still a challenge to identify the specific issues they should prioritize and those they should defer or leave to others.

In our sessions, we use purpose and impact as the criteria to identify these priorities. In doing that, we invariably find there is a set of priorities common to most CEOs. I've briefly set them out in this chapter and explored a few of them in greater depth elsewhere in the book.

Your principal responsibility is to ensure your organization achieves the greatest possible impact in pursuing its purpose. How you meet that responsibility defines your leadership and shapes the success or otherwise of your organization. The priorities for your leadership—the issues that you devote the bulk of your time and energy to—should all be geared toward that principal responsibility.

The key priorities in my experience, and arising from my discussions with other leaders, are as follows.

Hold the Vision

You should start with purpose. As the CEO, you have the responsibility to articulate the purpose and aspirations of your organization and to inspire and motivate all your key stakeholders—from staff to donors to peer organizations. You have the advantage (and responsibility) to look over the horizon in a way that other staff—focused more on the day-to-day activities—do not. As the lead spokesperson for the organization, you can convey clearly and powerfully the change you wish to see and how your organization will contribute to that change through its programs and activities. You can inspire your team by showing them how their jobs fit into the shared vision of change. Of course, others in the organization can also and should speak powerfully to that vision, as it is counterproductive for the CEO to not make room for other colleagues to be public representatives for your cause. But all who engage with the organization will want to know that the CEO is the holder of the vision.

Done well, your clear-eyed and principled commitment to this vision is a powerful tool for motivating staff, a key element of building culture, and a compelling way to engage those who are funding the organization, or who may wish to, given their desire to ensure they are contributing their resources to something that matters.

Lead on Strategy

In addition to holding the vision, the CEO needs to be in charge of the organization's strategy, as it is the template that determines how your nonprofit achieves its mission and impact. That doesn't mean the CEO should manage every step of the strategic planning process—far from it. But ultimately, strategy requires decisions on critical issues like your organization's impact goals, the trade-offs to achieve them, and the theory of change, so the CEO needs to be closely involved in those big decisions. The CEO is best placed to assess the consequences of these decisions on the nonprofit's work and carries responsibility for them. Of course, the board signs off on the strategic plan and is often closely involved in its development, but no board member will be as intimately involved with the work of the organization as the CEO.

Invest in Culture

Next comes people. The CEO must focus on the organization's culture, particularly in building an inclusive and impact-focused culture. The starting point is to model the behaviors that help create that culture. As CEO, you need to be conscious that everyone closely observes what you say and do. You should use this to reinforce the behaviors you want to see. For example, if you admit mistakes, it makes it much easier for others to do so; if you repeatedly articulate the importance of focusing on the needs of those you serve, others will internalize this; and so on. It's particularly important for nonprofit CEOs to facilitate a culture of psychological safety across the organization and within internal teams. "Psychological safety" here means a culture that encourages candor and openness. You also need to ensure that the individuals and communities you serve are centered in your work. This can be best done by building these behaviors (i.e., psychological safety and centering those you serve) into your culture. Given its importance to the effectiveness of a nonprofit, I'll explore culture in greater depth in the next chapter.

Focus on the Team

You can't do it all alone, and you shouldn't try. This can be a difficult lesson for new CEOs to internalize. They often think that they need to know everything (or give an impression of doing so) and show invulnerability by making decisions alone—as I did in the situation recounted at the start of this chapter. Nothing could be further from the truth. The most effective leaders work closely with their teams. Doing this well is a superpower. The team can be your senior leadership team (SLT) or, if you are a small nonprofit, the team of all your staff—or some other formulation. Other members of the team will know more about many things than you do. Given the space and encouragement, they will challenge your views and assumptions, and the end result will be better decisions. But this requires a culture of psychological safety and a leader who actively encourages others to share their views, as we'll see in the next chapter.

Recruit and Retain the Right People

Another key leadership responsibility is ensuring you have the right people in the organization. This requires you and your team to recruit well and, perhaps more importantly, let go of staff who do not perform or work effectively with colleagues despite support. New CEOs, and even experienced ones, spend inordinate amounts of time trying to decide whether to fire problematic staff and, almost invariably, when they finally do let go of those staff (having tried various other solutions), they will wonder why they didn't act earlier, not least because of the burden placed by problematic staff on their colleagues and the culture. We'll discuss this further in the Team chapter.

Work Effectively with Your Board

Boards have the responsibility to hire and fire the CEO and, more broadly, to govern the organization, so, by definition, the board should be a priority for the CEO. A good board will provide high-level support for the CEO while holding them accountable for the organization's performance. A dysfunctional board will meddle in issues of management, perhaps fight within itself, and demand an undue amount of the CEO's time. The CEO's objective is to make sure, as best they can, to have an effective and not dysfunctional board. While the board itself will ensure whether it operates effectively, all CEOs should prioritize investing in relationships with individual board members. The potential consequences of board dysfunction cannot be overstated. We'll look at the board in greater detail in the last chapter of this section.

Commit to Fundraising

CEOs need to lean into fundraising. Many CEOs, and particularly new ones, struggle with this. Sometimes they lack familiarity with fundraising, particularly if they come from a programmatic background. At other times they have a disdain for fundraising. But funding won't flow if the CEO doesn't prioritize mobilizing it. To my mind, fundraising is one of the most important priorities of the CEO because, without the requisite funding, your organization won't be nearly as impactful as it should be, regardless of the power of its cause and people. We'll explore this in greater depth in the Funders chapter in the next section.

In summary, the key priorities for the CEO are to hold and articulate the vision of the organization, lead on strategy, build an impactful and impact-focused culture, recruit well and let go of problematic staff, ensure a productive relationship with your board, keep those you serve at the center of your work, and relentlessly fundraise. Do those well and you'll set the organization up for success. How you do all of this depends in significant part on your leadership style, which is what we'll now turn to.

INTERVIEW

Priorities of a Nonprofit CEO at the Five-Year Mark

Observations of Mathieu Lefevre, founding CEO of More in Common, as the organization marked its fifth anniversary. More in Common's mission is to understand the forces driving people apart, to find common ground, and to help bring people together to tackle shared challenges. It draws from groundbreaking research to test and find solutions, working with partners that have the capacity to make a real difference at scale.

The three biggest priorities for me are culture, strategy, and funding. Much of why those are my three biggest priorities will be obvious: I imagine those three will feature in any CEO's list. So let me perhaps elaborate a little on the less obvious aspects:

Culture: Maintaining a positive work culture in the 2020s in the social sector is a real challenge. The last few years have seen our sector (and the world beyond) deal with a welcome and long overdue reckoning on important issues that affect the workplace: race and diversity, LGBTQ rights and discrimination, and many more. Those have prompted some internal conversations in the workplace which have led to much-needed positive changes. But too often in our sector that has led to an excessive focus on internal dynamics which have come at the cost of our work and our mission. Too many organizations in our sector have become entirely paralyzed by non-stop internal discussions on DEI and culture and identity. I consider it one of our greatest successes as a team to have avoided such paralysis. The main reason we have managed to do this is by recruiting a diverse team, and specifically one with different worldviews and life experiences.

Strategy: Expressing a strategy that works as an inspirational sketch and not a blueprint, enabling teams at the national level to function with great autonomy is a priority and not a job easily done. What level of detail should a strategy take in a nonprofit operating in different scales and geographies? How do you accommodate for different people needing different levels of clarity in the strategy? How do you draw up a strategy that empowers leaders to make decisions and gives them strategic clarity?

Funding: The greatest challenge here has been convincing funders to fund us beyond the start-up phase. Lots of funders want to fund a new venture but finding funding when you are growing and five years old is harder.[2]

YOUR LEADERSHIP STYLE

Your leadership style refers to the methods and behaviors you use to motivate, manage, and direct your team. Those stepping into a new role as CEO of a nonprofit often wonder what their leadership style should be. Should they be more unilateral in their decision-making, more inclusive, or something in between? They may be concerned that whatever style they have developed over the years in lower-level positions may not be best suited to their new role and responsibilities. They may feel that now that they are in charge of the whole organization, they need to stamp their authority more clearly. Or they may struggle with the responsibility of being the final decision-maker.

As you reflect on the style of leadership you want to bring to the role, you need to consider how power operates in a nonprofit, and what style best suits the objectives you want to achieve.

1. Power Is More Diffuse

Nonprofit CEOs also need to come to grips with the reality that power is often quite diffuse at their organizations—certainly more so than in many private-sector organizations. Businesses generally have a more hierarchical structure, with the CEO exercising executive authority.* In contrast, nonprofit leaders have to be able to exercise "soft power." This is because nonprofit staff generally expect leadership to be more consultative than would be the case at most businesses, in part reflecting the fact that they are usually more intrinsically, and less financially, motivated. They also tend to be more engaged with important social causes than their private-sector colleagues and will often bring their activism to work.

It is also because nonprofits have more stakeholders with significant influence on their work than most businesses do. For nonprofits, key external stakeholders include the individuals and communities served,

---

* A striking example of an overly hierarchical corporate culture was that at the Australian operations of the global accountancy firm PwC. An investigation into those operations following the misuse of confidential government information found: "Culturally, the generally accepted view is that the CEO 'runs the show.' During a long period of commercial success, this has translated to a reluctance of partners to challenge the CEO, even at senior leadership levels... In practice there is not a lot of constructive dissent, with relationships and loyalty being key to career progression." Edmund Tadros and Neil Chenoweth, "Profit-first 'shadow' culture blamed for PwC scandal," *Australian Financial Review*, September 27, 2023.

funders, and peer organizations, while internal stakeholders include staff and the board. The CEO needs to keep donors and board members actively engaged, not having direct authority over them.

The individuals and communities you serve will have their own priorities to which you need to be attuned. Some larger nonprofits, such as the Girl Scouts or Habitat for Humanity, have a federated structure, with many organizations operating under a common brand and in which the CEO's power over affiliated organizations is more persuasive than directive.

But even when power is more diffuse, good nonprofit leaders know how to exercise it in pursuit of their organization's purpose. As Frances Hesselbein, the former CEO of the Girl Scouts of the USA, observed: "You always have power, if you know where to find it. There is the power of inclusion, and the power of language, and the power of shared interests, and the power of coalition. Power is all around you to draw upon, but it is rarely raw, rarely visible."[3]

All of this is relevant to your leadership style. Where power is more diffuse, leaders need to lean into coaching and persuasion over top-down diktat.

INTERVIEW

Building Self-Confidence as a New, Young, Female CEO

Observations of Françoise Moudouthe, CEO of the African Women's Development Fund. AWDF is a Pan-African grant-making organization that supports the realization and fulfillment of African women's rights through funding of autonomous women's organizations on the continent. It is headquartered in Accra, Ghana.

I have been the CEO of the African Women's Development Fund for nearly two years. I started this job while the
COVID-19 pandemic made in-person connection virtually
impossible—and yet I had a short window to create connections and build trust with the team, the Board, and our partners and donors. I responded by making Zoom my home.
I spent hours in one-on-one meetings with folks, video on,
which was not ideal for the introvert in me. I had to find
ways to re-create the warm, informal, unscripted interactions with colleagues and partners that I would have made
in person. It worked out, but it was exhausting!

As a first-time, younger CEO, it took me a while to build
my own self-confidence. Having spent my first couple of
months in learning and listening mode (thanks to a two-
month handover period with my predecessor—highly recommended for leadership transitions), I had come to a sense
of clarity about some of the key priorities and the changes
that I wanted to make. Yet I had a hard time translating
them into swift action: it took me months to make some
of the changes I had identified in the early days. I think it's
because I wanted to take the time to demonstrate to my
team that the changes were not just what I thought, but
what was strategically needed, and get their buy-in. That
is critical, of course, but I overdid it. Sometimes, a leader
just has to lead. I learned that the hard way. As a young
leader joining a well-established organization that I had
been admiring, I have had to learn the difference between
respect and deference, and that it was okay to challenge
the way things had been done for years and years. It takes
courage and it takes confidence, but some hard conversations cannot be avoided, and some of them we must have
with ourselves.[4]

2. Common Leadership Styles

The business and academic literature have a wealth of material on leadership style. The classic formulations are laid out by the doyen of leadership and emotional intelligence, Daniel Goleman.[5]

His research identifies six common leadership styles:

Coercive leaders demand immediate compliance: "Do what I tell you."

Authoritative leaders mobilize people toward a vision: "Come with me."

Affiliative leaders create emotional bonds and harmony: "People come first."

Democratic leaders build consensus through participation: "What do you think?"

Pacesetting leaders expect excellence and self-direction: "Do as I do, now."

Coaching leaders develop people for the future: "Try this."

Research shows that the most effective leaders use a number of these styles—particularly the authoritative, democratic, affiliative, and coaching styles—switching between them as circumstances require. I won't review all the styles in detail, as they are largely self-explanatory, but I do want to talk briefly about three of particular relevance to nonprofit leadership: authoritative, coercive, and coaching.

The authoritative style is well adapted to purpose-driven leadership. According to Goleman:

The authoritative leader is a visionary; [s/]he motivates people by making clear to them how their work fits into a larger vision for the organization. People who work for such leaders understand that what they do matters and why. Authoritative leadership also maximizes commitment to the organization's goals and strategy. By framing the individual tasks within a grand vision, the authoritative leader defines standards that revolve around that vision.[6]

The relevance of an authoritative style of leadership to an organization focused on purpose is clear. I've certainly found in my own leadership experience that the ability to motivate staff around our purpose is a powerful mobilizing force: for my team, it's empowering to know that our work, done well, contributes to people exiting situations of extreme exploitation.

Of course, the risk, particularly for an inexperienced leader, is that an authoritative style too readily veers into a coercive one, often manifesting as a desire to control subordinates. I've seen that often in new CEOs (myself included). More often than not, this inclination reflects a lack of confidence rather than excessive self-belief and needs to be kept in check. Even in times of crisis, coercion is of limited use. It is not geared toward achieving sustained results or encouraging commitment.

3. The "Heroic" Leader

A version of coercive leadership too often found at nonprofits is the "hero" or "charismatic" style of leadership. If you have worked for nonprofits long enough, you'll have encountered this. These leaders bring huge passion and charisma to their roles. They are often founders who have created organizations in their image. But the problem with this style of leadership is that its important strengths—the ability to inspire others and sell a powerful vision—are often undermined by an overwhelming focus on the leader, to the detriment of the organization and its mission. There is nothing wrong with being charismatic about your mission and organization, as long as it doesn't morph into an undue focus on the self rather than the organization. But often the hero leader thinks that their interests and the organization's are one and the same, or even that their interests take priority. Such leaders often verge on being narcissistic, and frequently bully subordinates. They demand loyalty and compliance and oppose any questioning of their leadership—all justified by their belief that they know better than anyone else what is in the best interests of the organization.

This style of leadership carries huge risks, because it allows for little or no accountability for the CEO, even when he (and it's more commonly men) commits abuses—for example, by sexually harassing colleagues, or using organizational funds for his own purposes, or bullying junior staff. Given he is a "hero," and completely identified with the organization, any questioning of his behavior is regarded as an undermining of the organization.

CASE STUDY

A Hero and His Three Cups of Tea

Greg Mortenson appeared to be the real deal. When he got lost in Pakistan in 1993 while trying to climb K2, the world's second-highest mountain, he arrived (in his telling) exhausted and emaciated in a desperately poor village called Korphe, where the villagers nursed him back to health. In gratitude, he told them, "I'm going to build you a school." So started his humanitarian journey.[7] The next year he founded the Central Asia Institute (CAI), a nonprofit, which then built a school in Korphe as he had promised and, in the years following, went on to build and support hundreds of schools in Afghanistan and Pakistan. The work wasn't risk free— Mortenson reported being kidnapped by Taliban in the remote Tribal Areas of Pakistan on one particularly fraught occasion. In 2006, Mortenson published a moving account of his humanitarian journey and epiphany in a book called Three Cups of Tea. The book was a roaring success, selling about four million copies and spending fifty-seven weeks on the New York Times bestseller list. It became required reading for US troops being posted to Afghanistan. On the back of the success of the book, Mortenson started touring the US, making hundreds of public appearances in which he promoted the book, his story, and CAI's mission.[8] With all the publicity, CAI raised tens of millions of dollars in the wake of the book's publication. President Obama donated $100,000 to CAI from the proceeds of his Nobel Prize.

The trouble was that much of Mortenson's story turned out to be false or, at best, deeply misleading. Exposés in 2011 by 60 Minutes and the prominent writer and former donor to CAI Jon Krakauer were closely followed by an investigation by the Montana Attorney General's Office. Together they revealed that Mortenson had not ended up in Korphe after an attempt on K2—he went there a year or two later during another visit to Pakistan.[9] And the villagers didn't nurse him back to health, as he wasn't exhausted or hungry when he visited, allegedly for just a few hours. Nor was he kidnapped by Taliban.[10]

Even more concerning were allegations of mismanagement of CAI's operations and finances. It turned out that not all the schools Mortenson boasted of had students; some were being used to store spinach, or hay for livestock; and some had not even been built.[11] When it came to its finances, a picture emerged that CAI had paid the costs of producing and publishing Mortenson's book (about $367,000 in total), and had bought thousands of promotional copies of the book from commercial retailers and given them away. It had also paid the advertising and travel costs for Mortenson's speaking engagements, including chartering a private jet to fly him around. In four years following the book's publication, CAI spent about $4 million buying copies of the book and almost $5 million advertising the book and $2 million on private jets. Yet, despite CAI paying millions to publish and promote the book, royalties for the book and many hundreds of thousands of dollars in speaking fees were paid to Mortenson, not CAI.[12] This had consequences for CAI's mission—for example, in 2009, only 41 percent of the money raised went to building schools.[13] Throughout this time, Mortenson remained CEO of CAI, and a board member, and received a significant salary from the organization. He resigned as CEO at the end of 2011 and stepped down from the board in 2015.

What lessons can be learned from this sorry tale? One is the power of a charismatic, heroic leader with a hopeful story to tell. As Mortenson himself later observed, "Americans want heroes to believe in. Once the machine kicks in, you can be pretty much anyone, and people will flock to you."[14] If he had used his platform entirely for the benefit of CAI, instead of his personal enrichment, it would have been a more ambiguous morality tale, but that argument falls away in light of him benefiting personally and extensively at the expense of his organization and its mission.

Another lesson is the utter failure of CAI's board to hold its CEO accountable (complicated by the fact that Mortenson was also a voting member of the board—never a good practice for nonprofit CEOs). Holding the CEO accountable is a common challenge with overly charismatic leaders. In this case, while the board belatedly "recognized and agreed that Mortenson should pay some of the travel and promotional costs associated with his speaking engagements and books, and that he should pay CAI for royalties he received from books purchased by CAI . . . [n]either the board nor Mortenson, however, took steps to implement those agreements."[15]

And a third lesson is that this style of overly charismatic leadership will rarely be for the benefit of the community purportedly being served. In fact, the community often operates as a prop for the leader's efforts at self-promotion. As one observer noted, "[Mortenson is] the hero of his books, and he believes in scale, speed, and the constant need for more money and more construction. He shows no special knowledge of Pakistan or Afghanistan. In fact, he spends very little time in Central Asia."[16]

All in all, it's quite a sad story. Mortenson was clearly committed to supporting education in areas of the world where there was an overwhelming need for it, long before his self-promotion efforts took over his life and undermined his organization's mission. But his deceptions and CAI's governance failures did more than just damage its mission; they also exploited the desire of donors and other supporters to believe in hope and a powerful cause—and gave succor to those who seek to undermine the credibility of the nonprofit sector.

4. The Leader as Coach

At the other end of the spectrum from the "heroic" style is the coaching style, which focuses on supporting others, not promoting oneself. The leader-as-coach is rightly, albeit belatedly, receiving a lot more interest these days.[17] It is particularly well adapted to the culture of nonprofits. Goleman observed:

> Of the six styles, our research found that the coaching style is used least often. Many leaders told us they don't have the time in this high-pressure economy for the slow and tedious work of teaching people and helping them grow. But after a first session, it takes little or no extra time. Leaders who ignore this style are passing up a powerful tool: its impact on climate and

performance are markedly positive . . . Although the coaching style may not scream "bottom-line results," it delivers them.[18]

In my development as a leader, I have moved from being overly decisive and insufficiently consultative—as illustrated in the opening story to this chapter—to one who strives to bring more of a coaching approach to my leadership more often. I'm still a work in progress. But when done well, the payoffs are significant, in terms of more highly motivated staff and a more impactful organization. This shouldn't be surprising in a nonprofit environment, where most staff are driven in whole or in part by a commitment to the cause they serve and can best be supported by encouraging that drive.

So what does a coaching approach mean in practice? For me, it means checking my natural tendency to offer a solution every time a colleague comes to me asking for advice. Instead, I try to ask them questions to get their views on the best way forward, or why they don't feel they can make a decision or recommendation on this occasion. This leads to much richer discussions, and usually to better outcomes.

More specifically, it means:

- Working with your direct reports and other staff to help them identify their strengths and weaknesses, and connecting these with their personal and career aspirations.
- Helping them come up with clear goals for their work and a plan to achieve them, and supporting them in doing so.
- Embedding a coaching approach into the culture of your organization, along with the values of trust and accountability.[19]
- Being willing to receive and act on lots of feedback from across the organization.
- Staying flexible.
- Delegating when you can.

The coaching style of leadership requires a significant up-front investment of time, but the results are manifold: stronger longer-term performance, reinforcement of an inclusive culture and psychological safety, and "bottom-line" results in terms of impact.

LOOK AFTER YOURSELF

The risk for any leader, but particularly one new to the role, is that they are so focused on leading the organization that they fail to look after themselves. The job of a nonprofit leader comes with huge pressures. You are always acutely conscious of the responsibility you bear to the mission, to staff, to the community you serve, to your board—to everyone else—and you often forget about the responsibility you have to yourself. But if you don't look after yourself, you won't be as effective a leader as you need to be.

Your self-interest in looking after your own well-being is also in the organization's interest. However, many leaders don't see it that way and, in fact, believe that leadership requires them to demonstrate granite-like strength and infallibility. But that approach will increase your risk of burnout. In this section, we'll look at how leadership challenges leaders' own sense of self, and the steps they can take to better look after themselves.

1. Focus on the Right Things

As we've discussed, many nonprofit leaders, particularly first-time CEOs, find it difficult to allocate their time effectively so they can focus on the important issues rather than the seemingly urgent ones that are actually distractions from the core work. Everyone wants the leader's attention, and it becomes all too easy for the CEO to make decisions on every issue that comes to them, which guarantees everything will continue coming to them whether or not it merits their attention.

Many new CEOs micromanage due to insecurity or lack of experience. A new CEO, feeling overwhelmed by their responsibilities, may find comfort in focusing on tasks and routines they know well, even if these are no longer their responsibility. A former program director, now CEO, may spend too much time on programs because that is familiar and often rewarding work, and they find it more engaging (and less scary) than fundraising, dealing with board members, and handling tricky internal staffing issues (such as firing someone).

The problem is that the CEO is spending time on things better done by others, and *not* spending time on the issues they should be prioritizing. The result is an overworked CEO who has no time to reflect, and colleagues who are disempowered and unwilling to take responsibility for difficult decisions. As we'll see in the next chapter, how the CEO behaves has a big influence on the organization's culture. Overworked CEOs who are pulled in many different directions should also consider the opportunity cost. When you are busy trying to do someone else's job, you are not devoting enough time to your own. Or you are working far longer and more intensely than you should as you are trying to do two jobs at once, doing neither well, and creating a significantly increased risk of burnout.

CEOs need to be aware of these very natural tendencies and pull back as required. They should ensure issues only come to them for decisions at the right time and level. They should push decisions back down to colleagues who have responsibility for them. A coaching approach to leadership can be beneficial here. Instead of deciding for colleagues, encourage them to take responsibility where appropriate, and support them in doing so. Do this consistently, and you'll find that fewer issues come to you that should have been dealt with by your subordinates. It's important to remember that if you make good hiring decisions and feel confident about your team, you should trust colleagues to do their job without hovering over them.

Then, over time, you will find that you have more time to devote to the big issues and decisions you should be focused on, for the better of your organization.

2. Dealing with Loneliness

Leadership is a lonely practice. This can be particularly so for newly promoted CEOs, as their relationship with former colleagues changes from one of peers to one of boss/subordinate. Regardless of your intentions, your colleagues will treat you differently because of your position at the top of the organization's hierarchy. The gap can be greater or smaller depending on your leadership style, but it's always there. Many staff find interacting with their CEO stressful, regardless of how approachable you think you are. Staff more often come to you with problems than positive feedback. It's crucial to maintain awareness of this power dynamic, which is present in every interaction, no matter how approachable or transparent you may seek to be.

Over half the CEOs in one survey reported experiencing feelings of loneliness in their role, and most of those believed it hindered their performance.[20] Loneliness is particularly challenging during times of crisis—like a pandemic or in tough financial climates—as you add the challenge of dealing with these crises on top of all the usual CEO worries.

One way to reduce the burden of loneliness is to build a leadership team you can trust, and with whom you can openly discuss concerns. This doesn't remove the burden of responsibility but will lead to better-informed decisions. Using executive coaching can also help leaders navigate these challenges. Even in the best of times, leaders can benefit from having someone outside their organization to speak to about their worries and hopes; during difficult times, this resource can be invaluable. Given all the demands of leadership, there is a particular benefit in having dedicated time to talk to someone who listens actively and asks incisive questions, to step back from the immediate pressures, to reflect and think.*

---

* Nancy Kline gives a powerful exposition on this in her book *Time to Think* (London: Cassell, 2015).

I certainly benefited from being coached during the pandemic. In fact, I've found the whole practice so helpful that I've now completed an executive coaching course myself, and regularly provide pro bono coaching to new nonprofit leaders. The feedback I've received from them is that it's a very helpful practice. And for myself, I find that coaching others educates me as I seek to bring a coaching style to my own leadership.

If coaching seems too structured or otherwise unsuitable, you can seek out a mentor—someone with experience you value who can offer advice. Mentoring is generally seen as more of a top-down process, whereas coaching is—or should be—more of a two-way process. Both have great value.*

Peer groups have been another invaluable resource for me. Some of the most valuable advice I've received during my nonprofit career has been from groups of leaders in similar positions. During my time as a chief operating officer, I joined a group of senior operational and advocacy staff from peer organizations and found a trusted environment in which I could openly share challenges, failures, and advice. If something structured doesn't already exist, you can easily set up a small, informal group of peers. You'll be surprised at how many other CEOs want a trusted forum for honest discussion and sharing.

3. Mental Health

Nonprofit leadership is stressful at the best of times. Often there is a profound mismatch between what we can achieve and what we feel responsible for. Leaders often feel that the needs of the community they serve are overwhelming, and if only we worked a bit harder and longer, then

---

* "Traditional mentoring (or training or advising or consulting) puts in advice, content, information. Coaching, by contrast, pulls out the capacity people have within." Anne Scoular, *FT Guide to Business Coaching* (London: Pearson Education Limited, 2020), Kindle Edition, 16.

we could make a bigger difference, and perhaps close the gap. But if you are not careful, that thinking will lead to exhaustion and burnout. So, you need to find a way to keep your commitment and empathy within manageable bounds.

Even when things are going well, you are most likely constantly thinking ahead about potential problems. I know that even when the Freedom Fund is in a very solid position, I'm reflecting on the next big funding renewal (how we can maximize chances of it happening, and what happens if it doesn't come through); board dynamics at the forthcoming board meeting; how we'll find high-quality staff in a tight recruitment market; internal processes on diversity, equity, and inclusion, and whether we are making the progress we want; when and how to phase out certain programs at the right time, and the impact that will have on communities we serve and our staff; and then almost invariably back to funding (funding concerns are ever present for most nonprofit CEOs). Your mind is constantly preoccupied with things you or the organization needs to do. And that's at the best of times. During the tough times, you are probably in a constant state of heightened anxiety—even if it's not apparent, sometimes even to your conscious self.

In many ways, the CEO has a 24/7 job, because you can't shut away those concerns and stresses, even if you are highly disciplined about maintaining a healthy work-life balance. That being the case, you need to do a couple of things. The first is to maintain a sense of perspective on the challenges, even during the tough times. And the second is to find ways to help yourself be more mentally resilient and better able to cope with the ever-present pressures.

When it comes to perspective, on several occasions I've catastrophized about the consequences of something going wrong at the Freedom Fund, only to find either the situation didn't occur, or if it did, it didn't have the consequences I feared it might. A good example is of a big donor unexpectedly cutting all their funding. That happened to us once, with no notice, but fortunately, we had sufficient reserves to manage the transition because we'd been working through budget scenarios and ways to give ourselves a financial buffer against headwinds, even though we hadn't foreseen this particular situation. And that unhappy experience has been more than balanced by other new donors appearing on the landscape. These days, while I often think about the risks of donors unexpectedly stepping away, I'm now much better at contemplating this in a broad context of the ebb and flow of funding. COVID-19 was out of left field for us, as for everyone else, but thanks to our financial resilience, investments in culture, and ability to rapidly change our approach where needed, we could navigate that particularly tough time.

In terms of building personal mental resilience, it's hard for me to offer advice. Beyond keeping a healthy perspective on events, you need to focus on your ability to handle stress. That means acknowledging that stress is often present, and it's normal to feel stress. The worst thing you can do is pretend stress doesn't exist or impact you. Over the years, I've developed my own stress tool kit. This involves exercising regularly, trying (but not always succeeding) to meditate frequently, keeping work hours within check, discussing challenges with my wife, and finding ways to unwind outside of work. You should develop your own tool kit. The challenge is that in times of great stress, maintaining a regular routine becomes harder. When I travel too much, I disrupt my routine, often end up sleeping badly, and don't do the things I should do to restore some balance, like exercising and meditating.

Sadly, leaders are still seen by many as weak if they admit they are struggling with their mental health. This inhibits them from taking the action they need to get themselves to a better place. I certainly learned this through hard-won experience, including seeing a psychologist during a particularly challenging work and personal time in a previous job. That was one of the best investments I have ever made in my own well-being.

Each leader will have to work out for themselves how to recognize and respond to stress. The best I can tell you is that it's critically important that you do—otherwise, you will not be as effective a leader as you should be, and you and your organization and mission will suffer as a result.

LEADERSHIP SUCCESSION

One of the most important ways a CEO can serve their organization and its cause is to ensure a smooth transition at the right time to a well-qualified successor, ideally someone who will lead the organization to even greater heights. As a first step, this requires you to leave when the time is right, before your "use-by" date. Many CEOs simply don't want to leave a job they enjoy, even if they are no longer best placed to lead the organization. Some remain in place because they are nervous about finding a new role. Some can't contemplate anyone else leading "their" organization. Or they may fear that their successor will overshadow their achievements. Of course, all of this is the antithesis of purpose-driven leadership, which should be squarely focused on advancing the cause you serve and the best interests of the organization—not your ego.

There is no magic number on how many years one should serve as CEO. The metric is qualitative, not quantitative. Relevant considerations include: Is the organization thriving and getting stronger and having ever-greater impact? Are you still energized by the job and cause? Are staff still motivated by your leadership? Do you have the strong support of your board and key donors? For some nonprofits, the sooner the CEO departs, the better. Others have enjoyed remarkable success under long-serving leaders. While the evidence is limited, one study found that, although the average nonprofit CEO tenure is four years, the twelve highest-performing nonprofits identified by the researchers each had a CEO who led the organization for decades.*

---

* Leslie R. Crutchfield and Heather McLeod Grant, *Forces for Good: The Six Practices of High-Impact Nonprofit* (San Francisco: Jossey-Bass, 2012), 190 and Table 7.1.

Regardless of how effective a CEO is, the longer they serve, the more challenging the succession is likely to be, given that, after enough years, most staff, board members, and funders will only have experienced one leader and one leadership style.

When it comes to transition, there are some best practices to which all organizations should give thought. The first is a succession plan. This doesn't need to be a detailed written plan. Having a highly capable deputy (or deputies) who is well qualified to lead the organization on an interim basis may suffice. This will enable a comprehensive search for a successor (for which the deputy may well be a candidate) when the time comes. Even better if that deputy has had stints in leading the organization during times when the CEO has been on leave or sabbatical.

Another is to have regular discussions between the CEO and the board chair on your term and succession. The decision for a CEO to leave should never be a surprise—to the board or to the CEO! Far better to have an open discussion and, when the time is right, an agreed-upon succession process. An important part of that process should involve the outgoing CEO handing over key relationships to their successor.

Another consideration is whether, as part of a transition process or otherwise, the organization might benefit from co-CEOs. I've never been a fan of these, as there is a risk of discordant leadership, but some evidence suggests that organizations can benefit from such an arrangement, especially as many are looking at alternative leadership and power-sharing structures.[21] When done well, such an arrangement may well reduce some of the risks of transition, if one goes while the other remains.

When it comes to private-sector organizations, there is research showing that for the most successful CEOs, years eleven through fifteen of their tenure are "their best value-creating years": James M. Citrin, Claudius A. Hildebrand, and Robert J. Stark, "The CEO Lifecyle," *Harvard Business Review*, November–December 2019.

Leading a nonprofit is challenging and rewarding in equal measure, though for a new CEO, the scale will likely tip more toward challenge than reward. Key to getting a better balance is determining which things are most important for you to focus on, and which should be left to others. This requires a hardheaded examination of what serves the organization and its mission best, not what you are most comfortable with or interested in. At the same time as determining your priorities, you need to work out your leadership style, as this will help translate those priorities into progress. And you need to do all of this while finding ways to look after your own well-being so that you are best placed to lead your organization effectively.

Your leadership efforts will be greatly assisted if you have a strong team around you, starting with your leadership team (if you have one) and then the organization as a whole. A priority for every CEO should be investing in their teams. That requires you to build an inclusive and impact-focused culture, and to recruit and retain the right staff, which is what we will turn to next.

CEO ACTION POINTS

Determine Your Priorities and Style

1. Identify your priorities, which should include:
   - holding the vision,
   - leading on strategy,
   - building an impactful and impact-focused culture,
   - investing in your team,
   - recruiting well and letting go of problematic staff,
   - ensuring a productive relationship with your board,
   - keeping those you serve at the center of your work, and
   - a relentless focus on fundraising.

2. Understand how your leadership style will impact your team and implementation of the mission, and consciously choose the leadership style that works best for you and the organization, understanding it should be adapted as circumstances change.

3. Invest in your own well-being.

4. Have a plan for the succession process, whenever it might occur.

CHAPTER 5

The Team

Prioritize Culture and Recruit and
Retain the Right Staff

> *Good leadership requires you to surround yourself with peo-*
> *ple of diverse perspectives who can disagree with you without*
> *fear of retaliation.*
>
> —Doris Kearns Goodwin[1]

Despite my occasionally bruising experiences, the International Crisis Group was one of the most remarkable organizations I've had the opportunity to work for. And it was during my years there that I first had cause to reflect more deeply on the role of the leader in shaping a nonprofit's culture.

I joined the conflict prevention organization as its research director in my mid-thirties, straight out of US graduate school. I stayed there for nine rewarding years, ending up as deputy president and chief operating officer.

Key to its success throughout that time was the leadership of its then-president and CEO, Gareth Evans. Gareth was a former long-serving foreign minister of Australia and a preeminent global thinker and advocate on how the world could better respond to and prevent mass atrocities. He was a force of nature, and his personality strongly shaped the culture of the organization.

Gareth's leadership had many strengths and a few weaknesses. These were all reflected in the organization's culture. On the positive side, Gareth was an outstanding policy thinker and writer, and brought great intellectual rigor to all of our work. He had exacting standards and insisted that everything we produced be of the highest quality. Our high-caliber outputs generated respect from our interlocutors, such as government ministers and officials, and ensured Crisis Group got ready access to the corridors of power. He had an utterly relentless focus on our mission and drilled it into everyone. As noted earlier, we never had a written strategic plan during his tenure, yet every staff member at Crisis Group could tell you, without hesitation, that the purpose of Crisis Group was to prevent and resolve deadly conflict, and that our mission was to carry out field-based research, produce nuanced analysis and reports, and engage in high-level advocacy to policymakers and those who influenced them.

But, perhaps inevitably with such a larger-than-life figure, there were significant flaws. Gareth was notoriously impatient. This impatience often turned into irritation (and occasionally rage) with staff who didn't promptly agree with him or implement his directives exactly as he envisaged. As a result, few staff members dared openly disagree with him, somewhat restricting the flow and exchange of ideas. Also, despite Crisis Group having more than one hundred staff in the latter years of his leadership, Gareth never set up a leadership team. His leadership depended heavily on one-to-one engagement with senior staff on their issue areas. This was a continuation of the leadership model he was used to as foreign minister and isn't uncommon with think tanks. But it limited opportunities for him to test his ideas and decisions with senior colleagues collectively, and to get their buy-in and commitment.

Finally, Gareth created a highly demanding work environment, again in his image. He put in longer hours and traveled more than anyone I've worked with, before or since. He expected similar dedication from his staff. To excel, you had to largely abandon any pretense of a work-life balance.

What were the consequences of all of this? Without a doubt Crisis Group was highly successful under Gareth's leadership—it had an outsized impact in pursuit of its conflict-prevention purpose. He made it globally relevant and ensured it punched above its weight with policymakers worldwide. But all this came at a cost and stored up problems for his successors (with long-suppressed demands for more inclusive decision-making and a better working environment flaring up after his departure). Those who thrived at the organization held a similar worldview to that of the CEO. That meant that almost all the senior staff at Crisis Group during this time were white, native English–speaking men with graduate degrees from prestigious US and European universities. The culture was neither diverse nor inclusive, despite this being an organization that worked on conflicts in Africa, Asia, Latin America, and the former Soviet republics. This largely reflected the world of US and European foreign policy think tanks at that time. But, as an organization that prided itself as a trailblazer in these circles, it missed the opportunity to demonstrate how it could be even more impactful, particularly with policymakers outside Washington, DC; London; and Brussels, by bringing more diverse perspectives to the table.

Having said that, I should be clear that I was one of those who thrived under Gareth's leadership. I could put in the punishing hours, as I was ambitious and had no family for most of those years. I had a similar worldview and, of course, was a white, native English speaker with strong analytical skills and the requisite education. I moved quickly up the ranks and spent most of these years as Gareth's de facto and then actual deputy. In that role, I brought much the same approach to my own leadership, including the unilateral approach to decision-making that I highlighted in the previous chapter. And, for all the challenges, I remain deeply grateful for the wonderful opportunities Gareth and Crisis Group provided me with.

In the years since, I've reflected a lot on the lessons I should take from my time there. Those experiences and subsequent reflections have strongly influenced my leadership today and have certainly made me a better leader. I've sought to ensure that all staff members at the Freedom Fund internalize our purpose and desire to achieve the greatest possible impact. We endeavor to turn out consistently high-quality work, but in a way that is sustainable for our employees, regularly seeking feedback from them on how well we are doing on that and other fronts. We have a diverse and representative staff, while constantly striving to go further. I have an outstanding leadership team, where my opinions are regularly and thoughtfully challenged. And, most importantly of all, to my mind, we encourage a culture where all staff members feel included and free to openly raise issues and share their views, leading to more robust decisions across the organization. I'll discuss my efforts to create an inclusive culture in greater detail below and in the next chapter.

As for Crisis Group, its makeup and culture has changed significantly in the decade and a half since Gareth's departure. The current CEO, Dr. Comfort Ero, is a British-Nigerian woman, with deep and internationally recognized expertise on conflict. At the time of her appointment, the ten most prominent foreign policy and international affairs think tanks in North America and Europe were led by white men (eight of them) or white women (two).[2] Dr. Ero's appointment was celebrated by then Nigerian president Muhammadu Buhari (among others), who stated, "over the course of her career, Dr. Ero has worked as a strong voice in bringing the challenges of conflict-affected countries to the front burner and her new role presents yet another opportunity for her to do more for humanity."[3]

———————

In this chapter, I'll explore what organizational culture is and why it is so important in building impactful organizations. We'll look at how culture shapes the performance of teams within the organization, and what a culture of "psychological safety" is, and how to enable it and the risk-taking and innovation it supports. We'll finish up by examining the importance of recruiting the right people for your organization and letting go those who are not right for your nonprofit.

WHY IS CULTURE IMPORTANT?

Culture is a strange beast. Most leaders understand that culture is important to the performance of their organization as a whole and individual teams within it. But few understand exactly why, or if they do, they are not sure how to go about actually shaping and maintaining it.

Culture is central to the way a nonprofit works and its ability to achieve significant change. A good culture will amplify everything your organization does. A toxic one will derail it.

Given this, building a good culture should be a priority for every CEO. But that's easier said than done because culture is amorphous. "Culture is like the wind. It is invisible; yet its effect can be seen and felt."[4] You can't command and control culture. Rather, you need to influence and shape it. And to do that you need to understand what a good culture looks like.

Culture is "how organizations do things."[5] It reflects how staff act and relate to each other and how the organization represents itself to stakeholders, particularly those it serves.[6] Culture is endlessly varied, existing on a spectrum from empowering to toxic. A good culture ensures staff are aligned with the organization's purpose and feel supported in pursuing it. This is why legendary management consultant Peter Drucker regarded culture as more important than strategy, as reflected by the aphorism commonly attributed to him: "Culture eats strategy for breakfast." Culture can unleash tremendous amounts of energy toward a shared purpose and maximize an organization's impact.[7] According to one survey of 1,900 corporate CEOs and chief financial officers, over

90 percent believed that improving culture would improve the impact of their organizations.[8]

A good culture contributes to the organization's effectiveness in two main ways, one internal and the other external. First, it promotes cohesion within the organization. It encourages staff to have a shared understanding of how to relate to each other, i.e., "this is how we do things here." It reduces the need for direct managerial control and bureaucratic processes. A good culture improves retention of staff, increases engagement, produces more robust decisions, reduces unnecessary conflict, and helps break down silos (given alignment around a shared purpose). When problems do arise, staff are able to address them by building on a shared understanding of mutual respect and a willingness to find a solution together.

Second, the culture differentiates your organization from its peers. The right kind of culture helps attract talented staff, as well as donors and partners, and contributes to improved performance and impact.[9]

On the other hand, a bad or dysfunctional culture will be a drag on the organization's performance and may well lead to its failure. A toxic culture can be an existential threat to an organization. Another survey of corporate leaders found that a toxic corporate culture is by far the strongest predictor of industry-adjusted attrition and is ten times more important than compensation in predicting turnover.[10]

Dysfunctional cultures are all too common; we've all encountered them or have friends who have. They may not always be visible from the outside (in part because staff may be intimidated from speaking out), but they are all too visible for those who have to endure them. The organization may have a culture of bullying or discrimination or may tolerate sexual harassment of more junior staff. It may be mindlessly bureaucratic. Some organizations may have environments with limited trust, where staff aren't comfortable sharing their opinions for fear of being shot down. Others may be so inclusive of everyone's views that there are endless discussions and meetings, but important decisions rarely get made.

Nonprofits are not protected from having toxic cultures by reason of their purpose-driven nature. They are just as prone to dysfunctional culture as their corporate counterparts, not least when being led by coercive leaders convinced that the righteousness of their cause gives them the right to behave however they wish. Such organizations can be high performing for a time, for example, by setting unreasonable demands on staff, but they are not sustainable over the longer term, particularly in an era of greatly increased scrutiny of culture and leadership behavior.

CLAIMS OF TOXIC NONPROFIT CULTURES HIT THE HEADLINES

A toxic culture is not just a threat to an organization's effective functioning, but can cause huge reputational damage, as some of these stories illustrate.

- "Crisis Text Line CEO Ousted After Staff Exposes Culture of Discrimination"[11]
- "'Deep Regret' Inside Aid Organization Grappling with Sexual Abuse"[12]
- "Top Women's Rights Group Probes Claims of Racism by Staff"[13]
- "'Bullying Culture' and 'Toxic' Urge to Protect Brand Found at Amnesty International UK in Racism Inquiry"[14]
- "Review Slams Culture of Fear, Potential Fraud, Other Failings at UNOPS"[15]
- "Save the Children Admits 'Unsafe Behaviour' in Workplace"[16]
- "Audubon Society Hit by Claims of 'Intimidation and Threats'"[17]

Most of these examples share a couple of important elements. One is the big gap between the behavior in question and the organization's expressed mission and values. And the second is that in each of these examples, it was the leader's behavior that was transgressive, or the leader stood by while their subordinates created a toxic culture. This raises the question of how an organization's culture can ensure the accountability of all staff, from the most junior right up to the CEO. Key to achieving that is a culture of "psychological safety," which we will explore further in this chapter.

CULTURE IS MADE UP OF NORMS AND VALUES

We've talked about culture being "how organizations do things." More precisely, it is a "set of norms and values that are widely shared and strongly held throughout the organization."[18] Shared values define what is important to staff, and norms are the traditions, unwritten rules, and standards that ensure behavior is consistent with those values. For example, your staff may believe that diversity is an important value, but your organization also needs norms—such as a workplace environment that celebrates difference and recruitment practices that encourage diverse applicants to apply and feel welcome when hired—to translate that abstract value into concrete behavior.[19]

There is no template for fostering a good culture. Because culture comprises a set of values and norms, it can take many forms. And it will be heavily influenced by the priorities of leadership. Do you want a hard-driving organization, focused on achieving big results as quickly as possible (as at Crisis Group under Gareth Evans's leadership), or one that is more inclusive and supportive of staff and more deliberative in its work? Risk-taking, or risk-averse? One where everyone has a voice, or more hierarchical? Or a mix?

A number of studies, particularly in the corporate context (where most of the research has taken place), have sought to identify the values that are most important to setting culture. Those most commonly identified by companies and their employees include agility, collaboration, client focus, diversity, execution, innovation, integrity, performance, and respect.[20]

A nonprofit's culture will comprise a mix of these and other values. A "hard-charging" organization or team may prioritize agility, execution, client, and performance. A more inclusive and supportive one may prioritize collaboration, diversity, integrity, and respect. We'll explore below how the CEO can influence and shape their organization's culture.

PSYCHOLOGICAL SAFETY AND HIGH-PERFORMING TEAMS

In addition to your staff as a whole, your organization may have a number of smaller internal teams, ranging from its senior leadership team to geographical teams or functional teams (such as your finance and fundraising teams). Teams develop their own culture. Ideally, these various cultures are all consistent and aligned with that of the organization as a whole—as that should certainly be the CEO's objective—but it's not always the case. Just think of how culture can differ between the senior leadership team and the board. Or between an office in New York and one in Nairobi, or the more internally focused finance team and the externally focused fundraising team.

Given the importance of teams to an organization's effectiveness, a lot of research in recent years has focused on the characteristics of high-performing teams, much of it centering on the concept of "psychological safety" and a healthy environment in which people have the confidence to innovate and engage in healthy, responsible risk-taking.

Google's Research into the Perfect Team

In 2012, Google set out to understand what made the perfect team, in an initiative called Project Aristotle. Google had consistently been ranked as one of the best places to work in the US, and its leaders wanted to maintain this status. Believing that having high-performing teams was key, they conducted an exhaustive review of the available literature and applied all their analytical skills to the huge amount of data available on Google's staff and teams. They identified hundreds of its teams and tried to work out which characteristics were shared by the highest-performing teams. But they struggled to find common factors. Some of the best teams were hierarchical, while others were more collegiate. Some were diverse, and others largely homogeneous. Some socialized outside work, while others kept their relationships to the workplace. Some had more extroverted members than others. There did not seem to be any common mix of personality types or skills or backgrounds. Only when researchers started digging into behavior—i.e., "group norms"—did they begin to find commonalities between the highest-performing teams. The norm they found to be most important was that of psychological safety.

In its findings, Google concluded:

Psychological safety refers to an individual's perception of the consequences of taking an interpersonal risk or a belief that a team is safe for risk-taking in the face of being seen as ignorant, incompetent, negative, or disruptive. In a team with high psychological safety, teammates feel safe to take risks around their team members.[21]

Google's research also identified other important factors to effective teams, such as the dependability of team members and the setting of clear expectations for them, but psychological safety was by far the most important.[22]

The academic who coined the term "psychological safety" for team behavior, Professor Amy Edmondson, has described it as "a sense of confidence that the team will not embarrass, reject or punish someone for speaking up. This confidence stems from mutual respect and trust among team members."[23] It does not mean everyone has to agree with each other. In fact, this would indicate a lack of psychological safety, and that people aren't willing to express contrary views. It's not about being comfortable at work. Rather, psychological safety is about creating a culture of candor and openness.*

To promote a culture of psychological safety, the leader needs to do three things:

1. **Frame the work.** Explain why the work is important and, even though this may be a given, encourage the team to focus on shared purpose. To frame the work also means explaining that outcomes are uncertain; there is potential for error in the work, and that's okay—hence, it is fine to take risks. This encourages team members to take their jobs seriously and be more open in the way they approach the challenges.

---

* Amy Edmondson, "How Fearless Organizations Succeed," *Strategy + Business*, November 14, 2018, https://www.strategy-business.com/article/How-Fearless-Organizations-Succeed. Some conservative critics see psychological safety as a form of "coddling" of employees, leading to a lack of discipline and rigor. But this fundamentally misunderstands the concept. At its heart, it is about encouraging risk-taking, not closing it down, by ensuring that staff are encouraged to air views openly and contribute to better decisions and outcomes.

2. **Invite participation.** Show humility. Team members won't want to contribute if they think the leader has already decided on an answer. Ask questions and listen intently. Take the opportunity to openly acknowledge your own mistakes when you get things wrong. This lowers the costs to others of speaking up and reduces the fear of sharing contradictory viewpoints.

3. **Respond productively.** Acknowledge and express gratitude for contributions. Participation requires courage. Productive responses create a virtuous circle of participation when team members see that you are genuine about encouraging them to speak up.[24]

In terms of leadership styles, a coaching approach is particularly well suited to encourage psychological safety. As Professor Edmondson notes: "If the leader is supportive, coaching-oriented, and has non-defensive responses to questions and challenges, members are likely to conclude that the team constitutes a safe environment."[25]

What happens when an organization or team doesn't have a culture of psychological safety or, worse, where there is an absence of trust among staff? The most likely result is a dysfunctional team, even if it appears outwardly harmonious. For a start, staff members likely won't feel comfortable speaking up for fear of being criticized or humiliated. Staff will play it safe and not take any risks. You'll probably find a lack of constructive engagement, which may give an artificial impression of harmony but in fact reflects a fear of conflict. A lack of buy-in means members won't feel committed to outcomes or hold each other accountable, and results will suffer. Often, frustrations will simmer beneath the surface, bubbling up in times of crisis or stress.*

---

* See a short but excellent book on the behaviors of dysfunctional teams, and how to respond; I recommend Patrick Lencioni, *Five Dysfunctions of a Team: A Leadership Fable* (San Francisco: Jossey-Bass, 2002).

So how does a leader committed to building a powerful and empowering culture address these dynamics and put all of this theory into practice?

HOW TO BUILD A POSITIVE CULTURE

Creating a positive culture is a shared enterprise. Given that culture reflects shared values and norms, it can't be imposed by the leader alone. A coercive leader can certainly impose a bad culture—one ruled by hierarchy and fear and an unwillingness to participate or take risks—but that will ultimately be destructive to a nonprofit.

While a leader cannot impose a culture, they are highly influential in shaping it. From the day the Freedom Fund was established, I've been deliberate about the culture I hoped we could establish collectively, namely one that is inclusive and impact-focused. By inclusive, I mean a culture where all staff members feel valued and safe to express their views. And by impact-focused, I mean one where everyone internalizes our purpose and remains relentlessly focused on driving positive change.

I've tried to model the behaviors I value. And I solicit regular feedback from staff—which in turn has helped me reflect on my own behavior and adjust it as required. I seek to give "micro-signals" to colleagues in our day-to-day interactions, making clear how much I value them and their input. I do this in meetings, and in my casual conversations and chats with them. I aim to show through the way I listen, and encourage and respond to challenge, that there will be no retribution for expressing a professional opinion. I hope to signal through my behavior that what is important is impact, not ego. I am very much a work in progress, but certainly, I'm better at modeling desired behavior now than I was back when the organization was first set up a decade ago, let alone during my time at Crisis Group.

Here are some of the specific practices I've found helpful. These won't work for every leader, and they are context- and leader-specific, but they might help you identify behaviors you want to model.

1. I have an induction meeting (in person or remotely) with every new staff member of the Freedom Fund. In that meeting I do four things:

   a. introduce myself to the staff member;
   b. ask about their interests and motivations in coming to the organization;
   c. share with them the history of the organization (so we have a common understanding of the origin story of the Freedom Fund); and
   d. talk about organizational culture, and why I see it as an important shared commitment.

   With these meetings, staff are left with no doubt about the importance of culture at the organization, and their role in contributing to it. My hope is that this meeting helps create a sense of trust and accountability from the beginning. Now that we've grown from five staff in our first year to eighty-two, these meetings take increasing amounts of time, but I think they are one of the most important uses of my time, as they set expectations from the very start of the staff member's tenure. One former colleague in Ethiopia noted after leaving, "One of the most memorable things for me is that you are the first for me to get a direct induction from the CEO in my more than twelve years of experience with five organizations."

2. I hold quarterly "CEO calls" for all staff. Initially, I used this time simply to give quarterly updates, but I found that staff weren't particularly engaged, and I wasn't providing much that

I couldn't share via email. So now, on each call, a different volunteer staff member interviews me and is free to ask whatever questions they choose and to solicit questions from other staff in advance of the call. Given our staff work in twelve countries in a range of different functional roles, we tend to get a wide variety of questions and styles. I don't know the questions in advance, which makes it all the more interesting, and vulnerable for me. Everyone is invited to join the video call, which is recorded for those who can't join and want to watch it later. This format encourages me to be candid and open, and staff seem to appreciate the opportunity to raise questions about pressing issues.

3. At the end of the year, we encourage all staff to respond to two anonymized surveys. The first is on my performance, and the second is on the organization as a whole. These have the same questions every year so that we can compare performance year on year. They include a mix of multiple-choice and free-text questions. The results are shared with all staff and the board, along with my responses to the findings, including any action I plan to take based on the information received. The process is uncomfortable, as I feel quite exposed. But I think that the message it sends to all staff—that I'm willing to be evaluated by all of them, and value the feedback—is key to creating a culture of accountability. And over the years, the results have been positive. In the most recent surveys, the highest result was to the question "my colleagues are committed to doing excellent work," which scored 4.54 out of 5. It was closely followed by "I would recommend the Freedom Fund as a great place to work," which scored 4.39. The lowest response was on "I believe there are good career opportunities for me at the Freedom Fund" (3.48), in part reflecting the relatively small size of the organization, and very low turnover.

4. One of the more important things I have done as a leader is to build a close and cohesive senior leadership team (SLT) with

high levels of communication and trust. This helps ensure we have rich and productive discussions, leading to effective decisions. During our weekly senior leadership team meetings, we often talk about the culture at the organization and ways in which we can build and reinforce it. We regularly share notes of these meetings with all staff, to demystify the SLT and share the thinking behind major decisions.

5. Across the organization, we engage staff in key workplace decisions. For example, when looking at flexible working in our London and New York offices post–COVID lockdowns, we polled all staff on their preferences. We don't make decisions simply based on the number of votes, as there are usually other institutional factors at play, but we find the information highly useful, and a way of involving all staff in important discussions.

6. I personally engage with all staff across the organization in order to affirm their value and keep an open flow of communication. Pre- and post-lockdowns, this meant traveling on a regular basis to all our offices and program countries. During lockdowns, it meant scheduling one-on-one calls with each staff member, for each of the three waves of COVID-19.

7. I try to attend staff gatherings and celebrations. I want to show that I'm not exempt, disinterested, or inaccessible and that I'm interested in knowing staff at a social level, always within appropriate boundaries, of course. But I tend not to stay late, so there's space for staff to also engage without the CEO present. No matter how approachable you attempt to be, you can't avoid the fact that being CEO creates an inherent power differential. It's better to acknowledge this than be in denial.

The motivation behind these practices is to create and sustain a culture of psychological safety, in pursuit of our organization's purpose. They are designed for our organization and may not readily translate to yours. But the most important point here is not the specific behaviors but the value of being intentional about the culture you want to shape and influence, and identifying ways to bring staff along with you on that journey.

I've talked at length on culture because it is key to everything you want your organization to achieve. There is, or should be, a virtuous circle between your purpose and your culture, reinforcing each other. Nonprofits have a superpower: the motivating energy of a good cause.

A good culture helps you to be bold in how you approach your ambitious goals. It creates space for important discussions on challenging issues, i.e., issues that might elicit a range of perspectives and understandings within the organization. For example, if you don't have a good culture, discussions about diversity, equity, and inclusion can become disruptive. But a good culture allows the opportunity to work through issues thoughtfully and productively, and arrive at outcomes that benefit the organization as a whole and advance its mission—as we'll see in the next chapter.

INVEST IN YOUR LEADERSHIP TEAM

A CEO who builds and works effectively with a powerful team will always outperform one acting on their own. In larger nonprofits that team will be your senior leadership team. Of course, not all nonprofits are large enough to merit a formal leadership team. But, even if you don't have a formal team, you'll likely have one or more direct reports, who can make up an informal leadership team.

All the evidence from organizational theory and practice is that high performing teams produce better outcomes than high-performing leaders acting alone.* And the reason for that is obvious—effective teams give a leader more options and better information and allow them to test

---

* To give an example, two leadership books I've been reading while writing this chapter have the power of teams as the central thesis of their accounts on leadership. See Henry Engelhardt, *Be a Better Boss* (London: Whitefox Publishing, 2023); and Daniel Coyle, *The Culture Code: The Secret of Highly Successful Groups* (New York: Ballantine Books, 2019).

ideas and options and identify the most robust outcomes. Such teams have other benefits too. They make a CEO's role a little less lonely, as team members can share some of the burden of decision-making and allow a leader to work through their concerns with others invested in the outcome. Team members also help get buy-in across the organization, bringing their own teams along with them on contentious decisions.

Yet new CEOs often shy away from building empowered teams. Too often they are reluctant to share the burden of leadership, worrying that it will be seen as a sign of weakness and insecurity. New to the leadership role, these CEOs frequently seek to establish their authority by making it clear that they are the sole decision-maker. Or, if they have teams in place, they don't lean into them but treat their colleagues as implementers of their decisions, not fellow decision-makers. I understand the tendency, having been guilty of it in the past myself. But I can only reiterate that the most successful leaders are those who understand that tapping the strengths of an effective team is a demonstration of confidence and security, not the opposite. And one that will lead to better decisions and hence greater impact over time. I know that one of the joys of my role at the Freedom Fund is to have an outstanding leadership team with whom I can openly discuss challenges and fears, and thereby arrive at better decisions, with greater confidence.

HIRING THE RIGHT PEOPLE AND LETTING GO THE WRONG PEOPLE

To build really effective teams, you need to get the right people in place. There are three aspects to this: you need to recruit the best staff, keep them, and let go those who are not right for the organization. As the leadership expert Jim Collins frames it: "You start by focusing on the First Who principle—do whatever you can to get the right people on the bus, the wrong people off the bus, and the right people into the right seats."[26] Nonprofit leaders can struggle with this, especially when it comes to the firing of staff. But your organization exists to make a difference to those it serves, and that requires a laser-like focus on employing the right staff.

What do I mean by the "right" staff? Too often at nonprofits, hires are made simply by looking for someone with the strongest technical expertise or experience. But other characteristics matter, too, especially for roles that require leadership or representation. Would the person represent your organization well? Do they embody your organizational values? Do they have personal experience of the issues you work on? Are they thoughtful about what effective management looks like, and will they help to contribute to your culture and the success of your staff? Management abilities, in particular, are often overlooked in favor of impressive credentials or degrees, or a deep commitment to mission. But poor management can do a great deal of damage to morale and reputation and bring down an entire team.

Recruitment is hard even at the best of times. Many CEOs say it is their biggest concern.[27] Nonprofits have the added challenge that they usually can't or won't compete with the private sector on salary. But they have the advantage of having an inspiring cause with which to motivate applicants.

It's very difficult to know if a hire will be a good fit based on a round or two of interviews, a written test, their resume, and reference checks. Research shows that structured interview questions (where candidates are asked a consistent set of questions with clear criteria to assess the quality of responses)* are more effective than unstructured interviews (a

---

* Work sample tests are also good predictors if the job lends itself to giving the candidate a piece of work similar to what they would do in the job. Some jobs (such as communications roles) lend themselves more to this than others. Well-designed cognitive tests are sometimes regarded as an effective tool, but some tend to discriminate against women and non-white male candidates, rendering them largely ineffective.

series of interview questions that vary in nature and order from candidate to candidate) and reference checks and years of work experience.[28]

The reality, though, is, however robust your recruitment processes are, you usually won't know if you made the right hire until a few months into the job. And, if your new hire is not right for the role, your responsibility—once you have engaged in good-faith efforts to address performance issues or find a better-suited role—is to let that staff member go, in the interests of your organization and that staff member—i.e., to "get the wrong person off the bus." I often think this is the primary CEO recruitment responsibility. Given you can't conclusively judge performance in advance, you can't really be held accountable for flaws in hiring (assuming you have a thoughtful, structured process). There is little point in beating yourself up when you hire the wrong person. But you can certainly be held accountable for not taking action once it becomes clear that your staff member is not fit for the job.

Many of us struggle with this, particularly in the nonprofit sector, which often likes to think of itself as less ruthless than the business sector. But I don't think there's anything gentle about keeping on someone who is struggling, impacting your organization's ability to carry out its mission and undermining its ability to deliver for those you serve. Keeping them on is a disservice to them and your team. And while a thoughtful performance review process is essential, to see if the staff member in question can be supported into performing more effectively or transferred into a role they are better suited for, we often engage in endless processes to avoid making the hard decision to fire someone.

Moreover, inaction can have an opportunity cost. Retaining failing staff can demoralize other staff members and require them to spend more time than they should be compensating for others' non-performance. Inaction also stops you from getting someone better in the role. Some of the leadership decisions I have most regretted are not moving quickly enough to take action when I had decided someone should get off the organizational bus. I have felt chastened on those occasions when staff opened up about the toll of working with the departed colleague (usually their supervisor) and how they didn't feel in a position to raise concerns against their direct boss.

MOTIVATING AND RETAINING STAFF

Once you have the staff you want, the challenge is to keep them engaged and committed. A good culture is key, which is why I've spent so much time exploring what that means. So is intrinsic motivation, and this is where well-run nonprofits have an inherent advantage over their private-sector counterparts. Intrinsic motivation is the drive to engage in an activity for its own sake—driven by internal factors such as personal interest, enjoyment, or satisfaction—rather than for the sake of an external reward, such as a generous salary. So, working to address hunger and homelessness will be intrinsically more motivating for most people than trying to sell more widgets, for example. While it has long been understood that rewards, particularly financial ones, are a key motivation for staff, more recent psychological research posits that intrinsic motivation is of equal or greater importance. This is important, as most nonprofits struggle to offer the kind of salaries on offer at their for-profit counterparts but are very well placed to offer meaningful work. One recent US study of corporate employees found that 90 percent were willing to trade a percentage of their lifetime earnings for greater meaning at work. And on average they would be willing to forgo 23 percent of their entire future lifetime earnings in order to have a job that was always meaningful.[29]

Key drivers of intrinsic motivation are autonomy, competence, and relatedness. This is known as self-determination theory.[30] Autonomy is people's need to feel that they have choices and are in control of their behaviors and goals. Competence is the need for people to feel effective at meeting everyday challenges, demonstrating skill over time, and feeling a sense of growth and flourishing. Relatedness is people's need to care about and be cared about by others, and to feel that they are contributing to something greater than themselves.[31]

The importance of autonomy, competence, and relatedness can readily be understood when debating post-pandemic hybrid work. Many organizations have struggled over whether to mandate a return to the office full-time, provide complete flexibility to work from home, or something in between. The challenge has been exacerbated by the fact that, during lockdowns, working from home was the only option, so for staff who prefer that option, a direction to return to the office for any day feels like a reduction in a benefit already enjoyed. On the other hand, being fully remote can make it more difficult to build connectivity and a sense of belonging.

As we were working out the best approach for the Freedom Fund's offices in London and New York, we gave thought to not just autonomy, but also competence and relatedness. Many staff commented on the loss of connection they experienced when working entirely remotely. Many noted that their work benefited when they could come together in person as teams. But, of course, many also valued the flexibility that working from home provided, and the time they gained from not commuting. We polled all staff on preferences for a return to the office (encouraging a sense of autonomy) and most preferred the option of two days in the office. We settled on this, with a choice for all managers (in consultation with their teams) over which two days, and highly flexible hours on those days they are in the office. We've also sought out other ways to promote a sense of connection, through social events, off-sites, and learning opportunities to encourage a sense of flourishing over time. The arrangement is not perfect, but the outcome appears to have been welcomed and supported by most staff and contributed to ongoing high performance.

———

Having the right staff and a good culture also means having a diverse team and a culture that welcomes all staff. There is a lot to unpack with all of this, so we will devote the whole of the next chapter to this topic.

TEAM ACTION POINTS

Prioritize Culture and Recruit and Retain the Right Staff

- Prioritize building a good culture for your organization as a whole, and for teams within it.
- Understand that a good culture is one of psychological safety, and that is inclusive and impact-focused, and supports thoughtful risk-taking.
- Recognize the importance of the CEO modeling the desired behaviors as part of building culture.
- When it comes to recruiting and retaining staff, "get the right people on the bus, the wrong people off the bus, and the right people into the right seats."
- Lean into the power of purpose to motivate staff. Recognize that autonomy, competence, and relatedness are key drivers of intrinsic motivation for staff.

CHAPTER 6

Diversity, Equity, and Inclusion

Embrace Humility and Learning

> *It is not our differences that divide us. It is our inability to
> recognize, accept, and celebrate those differences.*
>
> —Audre Lorde[1]

By the end of its first year, the Freedom Fund had scaled from one staff member to seven. All our staff were white, and most had graduate degrees. Our board comprised one woman and five men, all white. Our staff, based in London and New York, oversaw our existing programs in India and Nepal and planned expansion in Thailand and Ethiopia. While we had a number of Indian and Nepali consultants based in those countries, it's safe to say that our staff and board were not representative of our society as a whole, let alone the communities in the low- and middle-income countries we served.

Only in 2018 did I belatedly begin paying more attention to diversity. Prompted in part by unfolding #MeToo scandals, my priority was to work with the board to ensure it had a better gender balance. I was not thinking more broadly than that. Efforts to improve the board's diversity were constrained by the fact it was explicitly a donor board,* significantly limiting the pool of potential candidates that could fit its financial requirements. Our efforts to make the board more representative of the communities we served started a year later when one of our founder organizations encouraged us to appoint someone who had personal experience of labor exploitation to the board and offered to make one of its seats available for this purpose.

By early 2023, the picture had changed. We had eighty-two staff members—thirty-five identified as white, and the remaining forty-seven identified as Arab (French), Asian, Asian (South), Asian/White, Black, Black (African), Indigenous (Newar Janajati), Mediterranean, or Parda. Nearly three-quarters of our staff were women. Over half our staff lived in our program countries. On the senior leadership team, we had three women and two men. One was South Asian, and the rest were white and from the US, Canada, UK, and Australia, respectively. In the organization as a whole, four staff members identified as survivors of trafficking, including one member of our senior leadership team. Our board of eight had four women and four men; two were from low- and middle-income countries, and one had personally experienced labor exploitation. The organization was far more diverse than when it began but was still working at becoming more representative and inclusive.

I'm recounting these figures to give you a snapshot of the Freedom Fund's progress, or lack of it, during its early years. Diversity is not just about numbers, but if you don't start to become more representative of your society and those you serve, then you can't take the next steps to become more inclusive. I share these details somewhat warily, as I'm fully conscious that talking about our halting progress on DEI opens

---

* In our case, the expectation was that board members, or the foundations they represented, made a grant each year to the Freedom Fund of several hundred thousand dollars at a minimum. As you can imagine, that significantly restricts the pool of eligible candidates for the board.

us, and particularly me as leader, to criticism. But I think many leaders struggle with how best to approach DEI, especially when they didn't think about DEI from the outset. I hope by sharing my own experiences, missteps, and learnings, I can help others better understand its importance and identify ways to help their organizations evolve.

Why did we take so long to become more diverse? Largely because this was the path of least resistance. We were growing in a hurry. In those first few years, we recruited staff who met our technical and educational requirements, without looking beyond those requirements to identify what other attributes were of critical importance, such as firsthand experience of the issues we were working on. Nor did we think to change our recruitment criteria and processes to expand the pool of potential candidates. We did not feel under any pressure to do so, because we were in good company with our peer organizations, most of which were similarly unrepresentative. When I started as CEO of the Freedom Fund, the four largest anti-slavery organizations in the UK and US were led by white men and had largely homogenous leadership teams. We also took comfort that our work, partnering with frontline organizations in countries with a high burden of slavery, was very much about supporting and shifting power to vulnerable communities. Progress externally allowed us to overlook our lack of progress internally.

Our efforts became all the more urgent following the murder of George Floyd and the rise of the Black Lives Matter movement. Our staff in the US and UK started asking what more we planned to do to ensure that our operations and culture were more inclusive, representative, and actively addressing racism and other systemic injustices. Our staff in low- and middle-income countries raised concerns about the need for staffing across the organization to be more representative of the countries we worked in, and to ensure that staff working in those countries received the same treatment and opportunities as staff in London and New York.

For my part, I initially felt somewhat uncomfortable with the pressure to do more. Like so many others, we publicly acknowledged the importance of Black Lives Matter and produced a statement about our commitment to DEI. I hesitated to go further, out of nervousness and uncertainty about what such actions would require and how they might change our focus on external impact. I took comfort that our staff surveys regularly reported high levels of satisfaction, and I thought that was more important than embarking on an uncertain process of internal reflection on DEI. I was also conscious that the board reflected a range of views on what action was required, and that we might struggle to reach agreement with the board on the best way forward, creating unnecessary friction in the process.

But staff continued to push for more, and I started doing more reading and reflecting on power and privilege. I came to the overdue understanding that we couldn't credibly tackle entrenched power dynamics in the regions where we worked if we didn't first look inward. I realized that we wouldn't be as impactful as we hoped to be if we didn't better represent the communities we served within our own staffing. Such representation—if done well—would enhance our legitimacy and credibility in the eyes of these communities and would also ensure that we had a deeper understanding of the challenges they faced and the outcomes they desired. All of that would contribute to greater impact over time. I also understood it was important to take action to maintain the staff's longtime support of the culture we were so proud of.

So, three years ago we began a concerted process and, since then, we have come together around a shared understanding of how to move forward on DEI and have significantly stepped up our efforts. I'll detail those efforts at the end of this chapter, with the hope that you will find them informative as you consider your own organization's DEI efforts. That said, we are still very much a work in progress. In fact, one of the things I've come to understand is that DEI is invariably an ongoing process, not a one-off exercise.

When you are a leader, DEI deserves your close attention. While you may believe your nonprofit is diverse, your staff and other stakeholders may not agree. You may think all staff members are treated similarly and have equal opportunities to progress, but what is *their* experience? You may be a very small organization and think that DEI is not a priority, but it will be to those you serve, and once your organization is bigger, undoing entrenched patterns of behavior becomes much harder. You may think that because your mission is about tackling power imbalances in the outside world you don't need to look internally, but you do. DEI should be a priority for any nonprofit leader. Done well, it ensures your organization is a better place to work for all staff and has greater legitimacy and credibility and, hence, impact.

I don't intend this chapter to be a full primer on DEI, and I highly encourage you to seek out the many excellent resources on this topic written by activists, experts, and nonprofit leaders. It is not written for those who already have a deep understanding of DEI, as I am still learning myself. Rather, it's intended as an introduction to the topic, for those leaders who are starting to grapple seriously with DEI. It will focus particularly on the role of the CEO.

WHAT IS DEI?

Diversity, equity, and inclusion is a catchall phrase for three distinct but related ideas. Diversity is about the presence of difference. Diverse here means people with different identities, experiences, perspectives, and qualities. Equity is about the process of fairness, a step toward full inclusion. Inclusion is about ensuring people with diverse backgrounds feel and are welcome in the organization. A diverse staff, in and of itself, is not sufficient; full inclusion requires that all staff voices, especially those from systematically marginalized backgrounds, are heard in important decisions and aspects of the organization.[2] Done properly, it should result in a workplace where all staff feel welcomed and experience a sense of belonging.

COMMON DEI TERMS*

Diversity: The differences between us—such as race, gender, sexual orientation, religion, ethnic background, ability/disability, language, and socioeconomic background—based on which we experience systemic advantages or encounter systemic barriers to opportunities. A diverse staff and board bring together people with different identities, perspectives, and qualities. However, having a diverse staff or board does not in itself mean that your organization is inclusive. For example, you can have a diverse staff but a homogenous leadership team, or you can have diverse members on your board who are rarely listened to.

Equity: Equity is about helping all people reach the same level of success, even if that means disenfranchised people are given opportunities (through tailored support and development opportunities, for example) that help get them to the same places that majority groups have historically operated within. It means more than equality. Equality focuses on the same treatment of every individual. In a perfect world, that would be sufficient, but people operate within broken and unfair systems, especially those who have any sort of minority status.

---

* Other common phrases and acronyms are: diversity and inclusion; equity, diversity, and inclusion (EDI); diversity, equity, inclusion, and justice (DEIJ); justice, equity, diversity, and inclusion (JEDI); diversity, equity, inclusion, and accessibility (DEIA); gender, equality, diversity, and inclusion (GEDI); and diversity, equity, inclusion, and belonging (DEIB). Definitions are drawn from websites of United Way, equity.unitedway.org; YW Boston, www.ywboston.org; Mission Met, www.missionmet.com; Public Lands Alliance, www.publiclandsalliance.org; and Bravely, workbravely.com.

Inclusion: While diversity and equity are proactive steps, inclusion is an outcome of those efforts. Inclusion gets accomplished when systematically disenfranchised people actually are and feel welcomed and experience a sense of belonging. This includes not just the presence of individuals from a range of backgrounds, but their voices being heard in the running of the nonprofit. Inclusion means diverse groups of people should participate in decision-making conversations and have available professional development opportunities and ongoing training.

Justice: This is long-term equity. Justice means dismantling barriers to resources and opportunities in society so that all individuals and communities can live full and dignified lives.*

Belonging: Belonging involves everybody, from both majority and minority backgrounds, feeling that they are a part of the group and identifying with it. It means more than just being seen—it means being able to participate in co-creating the culture of the group you belong to. Belonging embraces differences and learns from them. It is sometimes used as a concept distinct from, and broader than, inclusion.†

---

* In their more entrenched forms, these barriers are often called "systems of oppression," i.e., a combination of prejudice and institutional power that creates a system that regularly and severely discriminates against some groups and benefits other groups: "Social Identities and Systems of Oppression," National Museum of African American History and Culture website, accessed February 15, 2023, nmaahc.si.edu/learn/talking-about-race/topics/social-identities-and-systems-oppression.

† See, for example, john a. powell, "Bridging or Breaking? The Stories We Tell Will Create the Future We Inhabit," *Nonprofit Quarterly*, February 15, 2021, https://nonprofitquarterly.org/bridging-or-breaking-the-stories-we-tell-will-create-the-future-we-inhabit/.

WHAT IS A DEI PROCESS?

Being a diverse and inclusive organization means that a wide range of people with different skills, perspectives, identities, and experiences participate in the running of the organization. It allows you to draw on the broadest range of talent. It will give your organization greater legitimacy and credibility with those you serve, and with staff, funders, peers, and members of the public.

Consider the opposite. How will staff from historically disenfranchised groups feel in an organization that excludes them from leadership and the running of the organization—one where they do not feel welcome, where they often feel slighted or discriminated against? How will the individuals and communities you serve react if your organization does not include them in its staff or makes little effort to be more representative? How will other staff feel? What will this do for your mission, impact, and culture?

INTERVIEW

What Does DEI Mean in a South Asian Nonprofit?

Asif Shaikh is the founder of Jan Sahas, which means "People's Courage." It is a community-centric nonprofit working intensively in more than twenty thousand villages and urban areas of ninety-eight districts across thirteen states of India and supporting the community-based organizations across South and Southeast Asia. It works with the most excluded social groups on safe migration and workers' protection, and the prevention of sexual violence against women and children. In 2022, Asif received the Gleitsman Activist Award from the Harvard Kennedy School, which honors "exceptional leaders and innovators who have sparked positive social change and inspired others to do the same." Here are a few of his observations on DEI in the complex context of South Asia, with its caste system and the strong role that religion plays in politics, society, and daily life.

In South Asia's caste system, there is a group known as "untouchables," or Dalits. They are often discriminated against by other castes. I am a Muslim Dalit. When I first started this organization, I only wanted to work with Dalits, to improve their situation. But I soon realized this was not an effective strategy, because while many non-Dalit people discriminated against Dalits, there were many other non-Dalits who wanted to support our movement. It's like the civil rights movement in the US—even though that was advocating for rights of Black Americans, it did not call itself a movement of Black Americans or limit itself to them; it sought to mobilize everyone to the cause. We need to do the same in South Asia. This was also the belief of Dr. Ambedkar, founder of the Indian Constitution. As a Dalit he believed that all Indians, not just Dalits, had to work to eliminate this form of discrimination.

We also need to understand that Dalits are not a single group. In fact, Dalit is a manufactured term and refers to more than one thousand different sub-castes, and often members of these sub-castes discriminate against other sub-castes. As a Dalit, I often receive discrimination from other Dalits, for example. Some Dalit-led NGOs only employ Dalits from one of the sub-castes, ignoring all the other sub-castes, and hence discriminating in their own way.

In fact, South Asian NGOs working on issues relevant to Dalits often lack diversity. Many of them are run by non-Dalit caste leaders, even though typically their field staff are Dalits. The same problem exists with philanthropic foundations and consultancies—the majority of their senior staff are non-Dalit.

So lots of work needs to be done to promote diversity in South Asia, particularly around caste and religion. In our own nonprofits we need to recruit from a much wider range of groups and make sure that people from excluded communities are properly included. It is constant work. It is not just a good practice on its own; rather, you need to be thinking about it for everything you do. When you recruit a person, when you appoint a board member, when you select a geography [in which] to work, when you engage with any stakeholder or in any kind of activity—in everything you do, you should ensure diversity and inclusion. And not just our organizations—foundations and consultancies also need to do much more, too, if they are to change and support change. If each and every player in the ecosystem engages properly on diversity and inclusion, then we would be much better placed to change communities.[3]

DEI isn't a one-and-done exercise. It needs to be woven into your organization. The process of integrating it is a continuous one. Getting serious about DEI often requires changing and strengthening your culture, and leaders should be fully committed to the work, listening, and introspection it entails. Too often leaders who come reluctantly to the table think they can "deal" with DEI by hiring an external consultant, running a couple of all-staff sessions, and then ticking the DEI box. But this will not achieve any significant change, and it certainly won't change your culture. It may well prove counterproductive if the process is superficial. Rather, you should approach the process as you would with any important investment in your nonprofit's culture.

Similarly, nonprofits often make eloquent public statements about their commitment to DEI, thinking that might be sufficient, but it's not. Genuine commitment is proven by the investment of resources and energy in the process. An organization with good intentions can easily acknowledge how much it falls short, and commit to making changes, but then let those changes get lost in the long list of projects on the to-do list. This is especially true when nonprofits are under-staffed and morale is low. If DEI is siloed, treated only as a human resources issue, or handed off to a junior-level staff member with little support or buy-in from senior leadership, your success will be limited. Instead, efforts should be integrated across the organization, with all of senior leadership understanding that they will be held accountable for progress.

The answer isn't to simply add to workloads by asking for volunteers to take on responsibility for DEI on top of their existing roles. Only concrete steps will drive forward the process. This can include some or all of the following measures:

- Allocate space in your budget for expert advice, staffing, and training as necessary.
- Engage expert consultants, but keep in mind that consultants are most helpful for kick-starting the process and identifying a plan of action. In the long term, only your organization itself can carry out the substantive changes to culture, processes, and structures, and sustain the process of continually assessing progress.
- Shift workloads so that a senior-level staff member can take on responsibility for DEI and have the capacity to do so by passing off some of their other responsibilities to another colleague.
- Form a voluntary, representative, rotating DEI committee from among staff. Ensure that staff feel comfortable raising concerns or questions with those on the committee.

- Shift job descriptions so that one person on each team serves as a trained DEI focal person or, if your organization is large enough to warrant it, hire a full-time DEI staff member.
- Solicit input from across the organization to develop a DEI vision and a plan with concrete and measurable steps on everything from recruitment to training to staff development, and track performance.

THE CEO'S ROLE

The CEO needs to lead DEI efforts and do so in a way that brings along all staff and gives them an active role in shaping the process and outcomes. I've found that treating DEI as a key component of our culture (and not as something separate to it) helped me better understand that it is central to building an inclusive and representative organization. It has not been an easy process. I had long been one of those nonprofit leaders who thought that my organization was doing pretty well on culture, including DEI, and was taken aback when some staff asked what more we were going to do to make our organization more diverse and inclusive. It felt like a challenge to my commitment to positive change. And it was—as it should be.

The real test of our commitment to the values we espouse is how we respond when we recognize that our organizations do not fully reflect them. Failure to respond appropriately can turn this conversation into a challenge to the leader's authority. This is a fear of many CEOs new to the process, but the challenge to authority usually comes when the process is poorly handled, not as a result of the process itself. That's an important difference.

DEI processes can be particularly fraught for organizations when a big divide between leadership and staff already exists. Often leadership wants to focus on external engagement and impact, thinking that's where the organization can make the biggest contribution (and perhaps unconsciously or otherwise wanting to avoid tough internal discussions). Staff, on the other hand, may want to focus first on the internal manifestations of inequity—things like how a lack of diversity or unequal compensation impacts staff well-being. Their argument is often that the organization needs to "clean house" first before looking outside (but may also sometimes be more focused on prioritizing their own concerns over those of the community they serve).

CASE STUDY

How a Mishandled Approach to Racial Justice Issues Led to an Exodus of Staff

The divide between leadership and staff proved damaging for the Guttmacher Institute, a prominent reproductive health and rights research nonprofit based in Washington, DC. It showed how a badly handled process can disrupt an organization.

Over several years, staff on Guttmacher's public policy team made a number of complaints about racial tokenization, verbal abuse, discrimination by leadership against employees of color and people with children, and retaliation against staff who raised some of these concerns. These complaints went largely unaddressed by leadership.

During a meeting soon after the murder of George Floyd, these grievances came to a head as staff made a number of requests for internal changes to better support Black staff and other employees of color. Their demands included looser deadlines, better-designed leave policies, and more racial equity training. Leadership resisted these requests, arguing that the focus should be external rather than on internal problems in the workplace, and downplaying the direct connection between racist violence and the need for greater equity within the organization. A senior leadership team member became frustrated that staffers kept talking about "workplace problems" instead of "police brutality."

On the other hand, a number of staff believed that managers took advantage of the moral commitment staff felt toward their mission and allowed workplace abuses to go unchecked. Leadership's refusal to acknowledge and address these issues—and their insistence that those raising grievances were "self-centered"—led to great turmoil and eventually a significant exodus of staff. In the end, more than 80 percent of Guttmacher's public policy division left over an eleven-month period, including every caregiver and the only two staffers of color.[4]

This case is illustrative of the divide that often exists between leadership and more junior staff. Too often, leaders take the approach that if their organization is doing good, it must be good. They focus outward—on the community served, and programmatic outcomes, failing to recognize (or choosing to overlook) that their organization is not sufficiently representative of that community and other marginalized groups, or sufficiently inclusive. And sometimes staff (or a small group of staff) focus disproportionately inward—on the internal makeup of the organization and the DEI process, and don't give enough thought to the primary responsibility to deliver change to the community being served. Of course, the two objectives should be able to coexist and reinforce each other, and that's what a good DEI process seeks to achieve.

As CEO, you can and should play a critical leadership role in advancing DEI in a few specific ways: prioritizing DEI within broader organizational goals, balancing involvement with ceding power to colleagues, modeling behavior, striking the right balance between internal and external focus, and ensuring the process doesn't unduly disrupt your mission. You don't have to have all the answers, but you are responsible for creating the context for solutions. When we embarked on a substantive DEI process at the Freedom Fund, I was clear that it had my full backing.

But you also need to step back and create space for others. While you, along with the board, are the ultimate decision-maker, DEI won't be embedded in the organization unless you allow staff to buy into the process and express their needs and priorities. If staff feel like they will be expending energy voicing concerns, experiences, and ideas only for the senior leadership to intervene at the end and undo the whole process, they are less likely to engage. The best way to handle this is by supporting colleagues to lead the internal process. At the Freedom Fund, we established a representative DEI steering committee, with a high degree of autonomy and a remit to consult broadly across the organization, reporting in to the senior leadership team.

DEALING WITH DISCOMFORT

These processes, done properly, do shift power within an organization, and that can be confronting for some leaders. Sometimes, the issues staff raise may be surprising or upsetting to hear. As relatable as you may aim to be, problems around diversity and inclusion in the workplace do not always trickle up to leadership. Sometimes staff don't feel comfortable raising them or assume nothing will be done. Sometimes managers hide these issues from senior leadership in order to save face. Sometimes what you might perceive as a culture of positivity actually compels staff to keep things to themselves. And unfortunately, sometimes you might close your mind to these challenges, unwilling to listen or unsure of how to address deep-rooted issues. Whatever the case, it's all the more important that you recognize and acknowledge these concerns and issues, despite how far they may be from your own experience.

The process of imagining a more diverse, equitable, and inclusive organization often means considering changes to organizational traditions, structures, practices, and values. You may instinctively go into "protective" mode, raising concerns about how such changes would impact effectiveness, ability to raise money, relations with the board, and other practical concerns. I've certainly had to work hard to check my sometimes-reflexive responses along these lines. This is why the strength of your organizational culture is of such importance. A good culture will better support a thoughtful, ongoing process.

As I've also learned, the CEO's role—its boundaries or the fact of you occupying it—may be questioned, by discussions of things like adopting a less hierarchical management structure and the need for better representation of marginalized identities in leadership. This is when it is critical, as a truly mission-focused leader, for you to step away from concerns about self-preservation. Your ultimate goal is to seek what is best for your organization and mission, and to be open to change, if change means a healthier and more impactful organization.

All of this requires quite a bit of introspection: you won't be ready to lead an organization committed to DEI unless you are consciously learning and reflecting with humility. This means committing actual time and energy to read about, examine, and discuss your relationship to systems of power and privilege. You might choose to join a reading group or find a mentor who can help you work through these issues. While you don't need to feel like a DEI expert, you cannot leave the educational or practical work to other colleagues, specifically women and people of color, who are often expected to take on the undue burden of DEI work in the workplace.[5]

As the main representative of the organization, the CEO has a responsibility to embody its values and aspirations. You should take the role of modeling inclusive language and behavior seriously, both in interpersonal interactions and public communications, admitting shortcomings and being willing to be held accountable for mistakes and harms caused.

WHEN DEI PROCESSES GO WRONG

Believing in the importance of DEI is quite different from effectively operationalizing it, as we've explored above. Even with the best will in the world, embarking on a broad-ranging process can be a profound challenge.

A number of nonprofits have experienced significant turmoil during their DEI process, and some have even imploded.* This is not the norm, and many of those organizations, but certainly not all of them, likely had problematic cultures to begin with. Regardless, given our first obligation as leaders is to the mission and the people we serve, we must understand how these processes can strengthen our work, not derail it.

There are a number of scenarios in which addressing DEI can be particularly challenging, even for organizations with a healthy culture. In one scenario, fundamentally divergent views exist within the organization—from board members all the way to junior staff—about what diversity and inclusion mean. While DEI is about tackling injustice and inequality within our organizations, that straightforward declaration carries a lot of weight. To some it might mean issues of discrimination and different treatment within their nonprofit, such as tackling microaggressions,† reviewing recruitment policies to ensure a wider

---

* For example: "Closing Campaign Bootcamp," Campaign Bootcamp website, December 22, 2021, https://campaignbootcamp.org/blog/2021/closing_campaign _bootcamp/index.html; see also Ryan Grim, "Elephant in the Zoom," *Intercept*, June 13, 2022, theintercept.com/2022/06/13/progressive-organizing-infighting -callout-culture and Thomas B. Edsall, "Democrats Are Having a Purity-Test Problem at Exactly the Wrong Time," *New York Times*, June 29, 2022, https://www .nytimes.com/2022/06/29/opinion/progressive-nonprofits-philanthropy.html.

† Microaggressions are "brief and commonplace verbal, behavioral, or environmental indignities, whether intentional or unintentional, that communicate hostile, derogatory, or negative racial slights and insults toward Black, Indigenous and other people of color." "Living United: A Guide for Becoming a More Equitable Organization," United Way website, equity.unitedway.org/sites/default/files/file /united-way--equity-toolkit.pdf.

pool of candidates, and making leadership more diverse and inclusive. To others, the statement might speak to the fact that structures in our society have systematically excluded and discriminated against people of color and other minority groups, and their concern is that this is being replicated in their organization. And to others, a strong focus on DEI may feel exclusionary, and make them feel like they don't fully belong to the organization.

Our perspective can shape the language we use. Many will talk about barriers to inclusion as systems of oppression and structural impediments resulting from, or leading to, racial privilege* and white supremacy.† Others will feel defensive and even distressed by that language and the accusation (to their mind) of their active wrongdoing. And some, in turn, will be upset at *that* reaction, and see it as white fragility—defined as a defensiveness among privileged white men and women, which cannot be accommodated as an acceptable viewpoint. The reality is that the terminology used can carry a lot of weight and can't always be readily adapted to the sensitivities of all those involved. Often the most important first step is to help everyone involved get to a shared understanding of the language and concepts to be used, as a step toward more substantive engagement.

In other scenarios, there is broad buy-in to the importance of a process, but the process itself is badly managed by the board or leadership or staff or all of them, resulting in increased dysfunction. You can easily find many examples of such dysfunction, some of which are described in an *Intercept* piece titled "Elephant in the Zoom: Meltdowns Have Brought Progressive Advocacy Groups to a Standstill at

---

* Racial privilege is: "Race-based advantages and preferential treatment based on skin color (often experienced without any conscious effort or awareness), "Living United," United Way website.

† White supremacy is: "The existence of racial power that denotes a system of structural or societal racism that privileges White people over others, regardless of the presence or absence of racial hatred," "Living Guide," United Way website.

a Critical Moment in World History."[6] I have mixed views on these examples. I tend to believe that if a DEI process exposes conflicts in an organization that are powerful enough to derail it, then there is a good chance that significant problems with its culture (including around exclusion and discrimination) already existed, had long festered, and were probably undermining the organization's effectiveness in any event. But that won't always be the case, and quite clearly badly run processes, such as those that are focused only on difference and not interested in encouraging inclusion and a sense of belonging for all, can be highly destructive.

While DEI processes can be challenging and sometimes disruptive, that's not a reason not to engage in them. (In fact, "disruption" can often bring about productive changes in the long term.) Rather, these challenges highlight the critical importance of the CEO being invested in the whole process, ensuring the necessary resources and support are available and that a good culture is in place to help the organization get the most out of its DEI efforts. To make this discussion more concrete, I'll conclude this chapter with an overview of how we have approached all of this at the Freedom Fund over the last couple of years in the hope that some of this may be of use to others embarking on this process.

THE DEI PROCESS AT THE FREEDOM FUND

Every organization is different and will need to consider specific nuances of their sector and structure to best advance DEI. At the Freedom Fund, we started a multi-stage process in 2020 to identify what we needed to address to ensure our organization was properly diverse and inclusive.

Consultation: We began with an internal staff consultation process to collect the thoughts and experiences of staff through small group discussions and surveys. We analyzed the findings to identify themes and trends and presented them at a staff-wide meeting, during which staff had the opportunity to ask questions and share reflections. Key areas for growth fell into three themes: communication, organizational culture and values, and empowerment and agency.

Staff recommendations included:

- development of DEI-related policies and an action plan,
- increasing board and staff diversity,
- making decision-making and communication processes more transparent and consultative,
- addressing inequality between working conditions for team members based in our London and NY offices versus program countries.

Quick wins: Through this process, we also identified many changes that we saw as "low-hanging fruit"—straightforward action items that we were able to take up quickly—e.g., changes in hiring practices, increased support for employee mental health, and changes in formats of meetings.* We formed a DEI steering committee composed of volunteers from across the organization who serve rotating terms.

---

* We had good hiring practices in place, except that they didn't make a proactive effort to identify diverse candidates. To address this deficit, we revised job descriptions to remove unnecessary barriers (e.g., educational degrees or years of experience where not relevant) and to include wording that encouraged applications from marginalized groups; changed employment contracts to be non-gender-specific; continued to ask recruitment agencies for a clear breakdown of what they are doing to reach diverse networks and to challenge anything in our job descriptions that would cause a barrier for diverse recruitment; broadened our advertising market to include more inclusive notice boards, appealing to underrepresented and systematically marginalized candidates; actively sought to attract more diverse candidates for all positions being hired, including considering recruiting in program countries for what would previously have been "headquarter posts"; increased diversity of team members involved in interview panels for recruitment, with special attention to including hot-spot representatives; and continued to support our human resources team to attend ongoing external DEI trainings.

Digging deeper: We were pleased with the progress but felt we needed to bring in more expertise to dig deeper. We sought out and engaged a DEI-focused consultancy to take the process forward and help us build on what we had learned thus far.

The consultants undertook a process of learning about the Freedom Fund and previously identified DEI priorities by reading the materials from the staff consultation process and meeting with staff stakeholders from human resources, senior leadership, and the steering committee. They used all the feedback from staff to create a vision document that set forth our long-term organizational ambitions across all areas of DEI. They also conducted learning and development sessions with staff, leadership, and board members on key topics like power and privilege and having difficult conversations.

Vision and action plan: We worked with the consultants and staff to create a DEI vision for the organization—describing the kind of equitable, diverse, and inclusive organization we aspired to become over time, to which everyone felt they belonged. Most importantly, this included the significant representation of survivors and other members of the communities we serve at every level of leadership in the organization. We also prepared a concrete and measurable action plan for the next several years. The action plan will allow us to track progress over time and understand the specific policies and changes we'll be taking to live up to our vision for a more equitable, diverse, and inclusive Freedom Fund. We'll approach our next strategic plan with a focus on ensuring we can deliver on our DEI vision, among our other goals.

Board action: As part of its own DEI process, the board agreed to broaden the criteria for board membership so that it was no longer a requirement for board members to be funders, significantly increasing the pool of potential candidates. Then, as a number of board members cycled off the board, the board embarked on a global and public search for candidates who would collectively bring a broad range of experience to the board, including membership of communities most affected by modern slavery, lived experience related to modern slavery, expertise on issues facing vulnerable women and girls in our program countries, and governance and finance experience, among other attributes. The board also particularly encouraged applications from individuals who were based in Asia, Africa, and South America.

Looking externally: Our growing effort to integrate DEI into all of our work has also affected strategic decisions and the creation of new programs. We began to take even more seriously our commitment to advancing equity within the broader anti-slavery movement. This had been a focus in our programming from the beginning, which was always centered on engaging with and supporting the most marginalized groups in our core programs. But we also identified new measures we could implement, such as increasing financial support for survivor leaders through our Survivor Leadership Fund and advocating for others to do the same. We've launched Freedom Rising, a leadership program that specifically supports women, survivors, and early-career leaders to diversify the leadership of anti-trafficking organizations globally. We've also created an Employment Pathways Fellowship to provide opportunities for survivors of trafficking to work at the Freedom Fund.

We still have a way to go and quite a lot of work to do if we are to embody our vision of being an organization that is not only inclusive, transparent, and representative of the communities most affected by modern slavery, but also serves as a leader for better DEI in our sector. For me, I now recognize that good intentions aren't enough on their own. Leaders and their teams must proactively and systematically create new policies and practices to give effect to those intentions.

DIVERSITY, EQUITY, AND INCLUSION ACTION POINTS

Embrace Humility and Learning

- Recognize that just because your organization pursues positive change doesn't mean it is sufficiently inclusive, or appropriately representative of those it serves or of society more broadly.
- Invest in the work needed to ensure your organization is inclusive and appropriately representative, as this will give it greater credibility and legitimacy with those it serves.
- As CEO, lead the DEI process, but do so in a way that aims to bring along all staff.
- Internalize that DEI isn't a one-and-done exercise, but one that needs to be woven into your organization as an ongoing process of changing and strengthening your culture.
- Model inclusive language and behavior, in both interpersonal interactions and public communications.
- Understand that DEI processes can be confronting and disruptive, and that the CEO has a responsibility to help the organization navigate them in a way that increases the effectiveness of the organization, rather than undermining it.

CHAPTER 7

The Board

Invest in the Relationship

> *Boards are a unique and curious leadership structure.*
> —Anne Wallestad[1]

Nonprofit boards take many forms, often shaped by the organization's origin story and its purpose. A couple of organizations I have been closely involved with illustrate that quite starkly.

On June 16, 2016, Jo Cox, a member of the British Parliament, was brutally stabbed to death by a British white supremacist while she was on her way to meet with members of the public in her constituency. Jo was forty-one years old at the time, married, with two young children, aged five and three. She was a close friend of mine. We had first met in 2005 when she was working for the UK humanitarian charity Oxfam GB. We had celebrated at each other's weddings. Jo was the very first colleague I hired when I was setting up the Freedom Fund—and she worked with us for six months before embarking on her parliamentary career.

Following Jo's murder, close friends banded together with her husband, Brendan, determined to honor her work and legacy. We organized a memorial event in London's Trafalgar Square that was attended by thousands. Condolence messages poured in from public figures ranging from President Obama to Nobel Peace Prize laureate Malala Yousafzai. We then decided to set up a charitable foundation that would carry forward Jo's commitment to bringing communities together and combatting hatred and exclusion, particularly in politics. I became chair of the board, and the rest of the board (six members in total) comprised Brendan and close friends of Jo, all dedicated to the issues she cared about and her legacy. The foundation has stayed true to its mission. It has brought millions of people together across the UK through its annual "Great Get Together" street parties and community events. It has been active in campaigning for action against all forms of abuse and intimidation against people in political life, particularly women. I stepped down as chair in mid-2019, to be succeeded by another friend of Jo's, former British government cabinet minister Jacqui Smith. The board has continued to evolve, too, with only one of the original members still remaining— but all current members still have a close connection with the causes Jo was so passionate about.

It so happens that when I first met Jo in 2005, I was vice president for advocacy and research at the International Crisis Group in Brussels. Jo was in town to lobby us on a humanitarian campaign she was leading for Oxfam on the atrocities unfolding in Darfur. Crisis Group had also been established in response to tragedy, in this case by a group of prominent statesmen who despaired at the international community's failure to anticipate and respond effectively to the tragedies in Somalia, Rwanda, and Bosnia in the nineties. However, its governance structure was very different from the one we subsequently set up for the Jo Cox Foundation. Crisis Group had a board of over fifty trustees. This included eight former presidents and prime ministers, seven former foreign ministers, a couple of billionaire philanthropists, and a host of other eminent foreign policy figures. This reflected the founders' strategy to create a professional organization to serve as the world's eyes and ears for impending conflicts, with a high-profile board that could mobilize effective action from global policymakers.[2] Crisis Group quickly grew into a highly influential foreign policy outfit. Of course, a board with fifty members was far too unwieldy to effectively govern the organization, so much of the governance responsibility was delegated to a thirteen-person executive committee and other subcommittees. The board would meet for three days, twice a year, with the first day dedicated to committee and governance business, and the last two would bring the whole board together to discuss key global conflict developments and trends.

I share these two stories to illustrate ways in which the motivation to establish nonprofits can heavily shape the approach to their governance. However, despite the different configurations, all boards share the same broad governance responsibilities, which we will now explore.

WHAT DO BOARDS DO?

As CEO you are legally accountable to the organization's board, which has the power to hire and fire you. Implicit in that power is the responsibility for evaluating your performance. Other responsibilities of the board include signing off on the strategy, ensuring the organization is on a sound financial footing, and managing significant risks. As one leading governance expert puts it:

> Assuming the purpose of the organization is clear, the role of the board ought to be to ensure the organization has the right strategy, resources and governance to achieve this purpose in the context it operates in.[3]

As noted above, nonprofit boards take many forms.* Some are composed of founders of the organization or friends and colleagues of the founder. Some are donor boards, comprising the main funders of the

---

* Board members are often called directors or trustees.

organization. Some will be expert boards, with board members having subject matter knowledge on the issues your nonprofit works on (e.g., medical experts for health nonprofits), deep familiarity with the needs of the community in which you work, or other relevant technical expertise (such as legal, financial, or communications). Many are a mix of all of these. Some boards will be diverse and have strong representation of the communities they serve, but many do not. While the board has formal responsibility for appointing new board members, the CEO and colleagues usually play a leading role in the identification of candidates, and their induction, once appointed.

Despite their central role, nonprofit board members are almost invariably volunteers. The board may meet quarterly or more or less frequently* but, however often they meet, board members will engage with the organization a fraction of the time the CEO and other staff members do. There is a real information asymmetry between board members and the CEO. Therefore, the CEO needs to make sure all board members have the information they need to carry out their role effectively and support them in doing so. At the very least, you should ensure new board members go through an induction process to familiarize them with the organization's work, strategy, and senior leadership team. Thereafter, the CEO should do their best to ensure that all board members are actively engaged and fulfilling their responsibilities.

At this same time, the CEO should ensure that a clear demarcation exists between the roles of the board and CEO, and that the board doesn't overstep its role and start managing staff. The board should engage in governance, not management.

---

* In the US, the Internal Revenue Service requires boards of 501(c)(3) organizations to meet at least once a year.

THE CEO'S RELATIONSHIP WITH THE BOARD

The relationship between a CEO and the board is of critical importance, and sometimes fraught. Ideally, the board is cohesive, with a clear understanding of its role and responsibilities. The board chair is the primary interlocutor between the board and the CEO. That relationship is key, and, given its importance, one that every CEO should invest in.

At their best, boards—led by the chair—will support the CEO and the leadership team in carrying out their responsibilities, while also ensuring a degree of scrutiny of those matters that properly fall within the board's purview (strategy, resources, and governance). A high-functioning board is a huge advantage for any nonprofit, and key to ensuring the organization is well positioned to have maximum impact. Given this importance, CEOs should lean into their power to influence the appointment of board members, identifying and proposing suitably qualified and dedicated candidates, helping build a pipeline of potential candidates, and inducting new board members into the organization's work and culture.

But a lot can go wrong, and a breakdown in the relationship between the board and the CEO, or within the board itself, can be damaging to the work of a nonprofit, sometimes fatally so. One group of experts outlined potential problems in this way:

> Only the most uncommon of nonprofit boards functions as it should by harnessing the collective efforts of accomplished individuals to advance the institution's mission and long-term welfare. A board's contribution is meant to be strategic, the joint product of talented people brought together to apply their knowledge and experience to the major challenges facing the institution.
>
> What happens instead? Nonprofit boards are often little more than a collection of high-powered people engaged in low-level activities. Why? The reasons are myriad. Sometimes the board is stymied by a chief executive who fears a strong board

and hoards information, seeking the board's approval at the last moment. Sometimes board members lack sufficient understanding of the work of the institution and avoid dealing with issues requiring specialized knowledge. Individual board members may not bring themselves fully to the task of governance, because board membership generally carries little personal accountability. And often the powerful individuals who make up the board are unpracticed in working as members of a team.[4]

Key to the effective functioning of a nonprofit is the board's confidence in the CEO, and the board's collective and collegial performance. If a board loses confidence in a CEO (rightly or not), it has the power to remove them. And dysfunction within a board can be debilitating for an organization, as it turns in on itself rather than focusing on supporting the CEO and staff in carrying out the organization's mission. In such a situation, the CEO can spend a disproportionate amount of time engaging with the board members and trying to rebuild relationships and cohesion. While that's important, given the centrality of the board, it can be a big distraction from the other issues the CEO should be focused on.

My principal advice to a CEO is to never take the board relationship for granted, and to invest heavily in all board relationships, particularly with the chair. Proactive engagement will reduce the chances of board dysfunction, though obviously other factors beyond the CEO's control (such as the board members' own priorities, motivations, interpersonal skills, and commitment to the organization and its mission) will play a role. In my case, I have fortnightly calls with our board chair, and I try to meet or have a call with other board members every month or six weeks if they are open to it—as most are. We invite board members on a trip each year to one of our country programs, and I always participate in these trips, as there is no better way to spend quality time with board members than when learning about the work firsthand together. We invite board members to events we host or take part in within their vicinity. I'm also keenly aware of the anti-slavery work that board members engage in outside of the Freedom Fund (as donors or foundation program staff) and seek to ensure we can support and align with that work wherever possible. None of this is rocket science; rather, it's a recognition that board members are committed to your organization's mission and success, and the more you invest in the relationship, the better chance they will play a constructive and effective role in the organization's governance.

My other piece of key advice is that a CEO should never be a voting member of their organization's board. It is fine for them to be a non-voting board member—though my preference is that they not be on the board at all, but have the right to attend and participate in all board discussions (unless that discussion is about them and needs to be conducted without their participation). They certainly should not chair the board. The reason for all of this should be obvious, namely that it makes it extremely difficult for the board to hold the CEO properly accountable for performance if the CEO is also a voting board member, let alone the chair. It unnecessarily increases the risk of actual or perceived conflicts of interest—such as when determining the CEO's salary—and reduces the effectiveness of the board's oversight role.*

THE OVERLY DOMINANT CEO

Sometimes the problem is not dysfunctional boards, but an overly dominant CEO. This can happen with highly charismatic CEOs or with

---

* The nonprofit governance organization BoardSource recommends: "Chief Executive Serving on the Board. The chief executive should be an ex officio, non-voting member of the board. The chief executive's input in board meeting deliberation is instrumental and invaluable for informed decision making. However, to avoid actual or perceived conflicts of interest, questions concerning accountability, or blurring the line between oversight and execution, chief executives should be non-voting members of the board, unless not permitted by law." See "Recommended Governance Practices," BoardSource, accessed July 25, 2023, https://boardsource.org/wp -content/uploads/2016/10/Recommended-Gov-Practices.pdf.

founder-led organizations, where the CEO has effectively appointed most of the board members, who in turn largely defer to that CEO (e.g., with Greg Mortenson and the Central Asia Institute outlined earlier). The risk here is of insufficient accountability for the CEO, if any at all. This is not only contrary to the board members' responsibilities but may well lead to overreach by the CEO and unacceptable risks for the organization.

CASE STUDY

A Weak Board Fails to Hold a CEO Accountable for Alleged Harassment

In 2018, multiple women working for the Humane Society of the United States, whose mission is "to end suffering for all animals," came forward with allegations that the then-CEO, Wayne Pacelle, had sexually harassed them.[5] The allegations dated back as far as 2005. Pacelle denied the claims. The organization's board commissioned an outside investigation into Pacelle's conduct but abruptly called it off as soon as details were leaked to the media. The board continued to stand by Pacelle and voted to keep him on the job, though he soon resigned due to pressure from staff and donors. These were not the only allegations against the organization's leadership. Paul Shapiro, a vice president, was accused of sexual harassment by six women in 2016.[6] In response, he transferred to another position within the organization.

Board members were not held accountable for apparent leadership failures, with many of Pacelle's defenders continuing to serve. The board subsequently conducted a "reconciliation process" in which an outside mediator interviewed over 120 staff, but it refused to share the findings. Following the reconciliation process, the new co-chairs of the Humane Society board wrote:

> Our problems were far greater than what was publicly discussed in early 2018. There were more victims of abuse, harassment and other inappropriate workplace behavior than had previously been known, and there were more bad actors involved as well . . . It is also clear that the Board struggled to find its way through the situation and in many ways came up short. We let the organization down and, more importantly, let down the women who were the targets of these inexcusable acts. We failed the organization.[7]

Regardless of circumstances, the nature of nonprofit board/CEO relationships is, if not unique, then highly unusual. Volunteer board members, who engage with the work of the organizations on a very part-time basis, have significant power over the CEO and the organization as a whole. This really hits me when I wear a board hat, as I have done at many nonprofits over the years. I'm very mindful of the knowledge gap, which is almost invariably in inverse proportion to the power gap. It's not ideal. When I talk to other CEOs, their relationship with their boards is up there with fundraising as the issue that causes them the most stress. But, as has been said about democracy, it's the worst form of governance except for all the alternatives. There is a very real need for an accountability structure for nonprofits, and I struggle to think of a way to do it better. That being the case, the obligation of boards and nonprofit leadership is to invest in the relationship to make it work as well as possible to advance an organization's purpose and impact.

———

And with that, we come to the end of this section on "people." We've examined the roles of the CEO, staff, and the board and the way in which culture—including diversity, equity, and inclusion—is so key to the effective operation of the organization as a whole. As always, the golden thread running through this analysis is the importance of purpose, which provides not only the direction of travel but much of the intrinsic motivation that enables well-led nonprofits to be hugely impactful.

———

We'll now turn to your organization's partners. These are your external stakeholders, such as those you serve, your funders, and peer organizations and networks. The people and communities, in particular, should be central to everything you do, and we'll consider what this means in some detail. But all these partners are key to your organization amplifying and scaling its impact.

BOARD ACTION POINTS

Invest in the Relationship

- Prioritize your relationships with your board members, particularly your chair.
- Appreciate that your engagement can help promote, though not guarantee, board cohesion and focus.
- Ensure that the board concentrates on governance and doesn't get overly involved in management.
- Don't be an overly dominant CEO.
- Internalize the importance of accountability for your and the organization's performance.

PARTNERS

Mobilize External Stakeholders

Alone we can do so little; together we can do so much.

—Helen Keller[1]

The Freedom Fund's origin story is a compelling example of the power of collaboration. In early 2013, there were three significant, privately funded efforts against slavery. Each was being driven and financially supported by its own group of philanthropists. The first, Walk Free, had been founded by Australian billionaire philanthropists Andrew and Nicola Forrest and their daughter Grace Forrest. I was the CEO of Walk Free at the time. Our focus was on producing the world's first global slavery index[2] and building an online movement of activists around the world. The second was backed by the Legatum Group, a Dubai-based private investment firm with a strong free-markets philosophy and a deep commitment to supporting clusters of community-based organizations to drive community-level change. The third was Humanity United, the progressive human rights foundation founded by American billionaire philanthropists Pierre and Pam Omidyar. Its primary focus was on forced labor in global supply chains.

Somewhat remarkably, these philanthropists—each with quite different worldviews and strategies for tackling slavery—recognized that there was a need for greater coordination and collaboration across the anti-slavery space. Sufficient trust and respect existed between the philanthropists and the leadership of their foundations to support productive discussions. The result was the creation of a new organization, the Freedom Fund, which would be tasked with developing a new strategy to combat slavery and help bring greater cohesion across the anti-slavery space. Each group of philanthropists committed significant multi-year funding to the new initiative. Following a global search, I was very pleased to become the Freedom Fund's first CEO.

While we started the organization from scratch (as recounted in the Introduction), the Freedom Fund had the benefit of the financial and public support of these three backers, which gave it considerable momentum from the beginning. It also benefited from partnerships and relationships these funders had already established with local grassroots groups in India and Nepal. As a result, we were able to incorporate local communities' input into the early design and strategy of the organization when we launched our initial programs in these countries. After their initial five-year commitment, each of the funder groups renewed their financial support for the Freedom Fund, and all are ongoing funders. To date, the collaboration has withstood nine years of intensive engagement and impact.

The Freedom Fund's origin story provides a powerful illustration of the power of partnership. It's a highly unusual example of how some of the world's leading philanthropists subsumed their desire to do things their own way and came together to create a new organization, over which none of them had majority control, and which would design and embark on an entirely new strategy to tackle modern slavery. While

philanthropists often push for greater collaboration between nonprofits they support, they rarely have the same enthusiasm (or incentive) to
collaborate themselves with their peer funders. But when they do, the
results can be transformative.

Partners are central to effectiveness for nonprofits. Your most important
partners are the individuals and communities you serve. Some may quib-
ble at calling them partners, but to my mind, this is the only way to view
the relationship. You depend on each other. Your organization may wield
considerably more power than those you serve, but without them you have
no purpose and no impact. Also, treating them as partners leads to healthier interactions, better-informed programming, and better outcomes.

Your funders are another core constituency. Without adequate
funding, the most powerful mission and strategy will come to naught.
Here again, some may balk at labeling this a partnership, particularly
as power here is reversed, with the funders (particularly philanthropists
and governments) generally wielding significant power over those they
fund. But this is a partnership. Your organization and its impactful work
provide your funders with a very tangible way to make a difference and
contribute to the public good. That's of great benefit to funders, who,
after all, are providing funding because they want to help drive change.
We'll look at ways that relationship can be strengthened to the benefit
of both.

A third category of partners consists of peer organizations and networks, which are working on similar or overlapping issues to those of
your organization. Most nonprofits give too little thought to collaborating with peers, often because peers are seen as competitors for funding or
attention. But almost invariably, much more can be achieved by aligning
other actors to your cause than by acting alone. And the most effective
way to create alignment and scale impact is to collaborate closely with
peers and networks—which we will explore in the final chapter.

CHAPTER 8

The People and Communities You Serve

Ensure They Are at the Center

> *Life's most persistent and urgent question is: What are you doing for others?*
>
> —Martin Luther King Jr.[1]

A few years ago the United Nations Security Council held its first-ever session on modern slavery and human trafficking, and I was invited to give a briefing to its members. The session was held in the striking Council Chamber in the UN building in New York. With a monumental painted mural overlooking an impressive horseshoe-shaped table, this is the beating heart of the United Nations. Fifteen ambassadors sat around the table, along with the heads of a few UN agencies, me, and one other non-UN speaker: Nadia Murad, a young Yazidi woman from Iraq. I made my presentation, and then it was Nadia's turn to address the Council ambassadors. She spoke with a quiet dignity as she gave a heartrending account of how ISIS fighters captured her village in Sinjar, murdered several of her brothers, and committed unspeakable abuses against her and her sisters, including selling them into sexual servitude.[2]

Nadia's testimony was compelling and distressing, and I watched as usually inscrutable ambassadors were visibly moved by her account. But Nadia wasn't there to simply share her experience; she had concrete demands for action from the United Nations and member states. She made a powerful case for substantive measures they could take to help address the plight of the Yazidi people, and particularly the women and girls who had been so horrendously abused by ISIS. Within a couple of years, many of those measures had been implemented.

Three years later, Nadia was awarded the Nobel Peace Prize. Ever since, she has used her global platform to advocate powerfully on behalf of Yazidi women and girls, and more broadly against genocide and sexual violence. She founded Nadia's Initiative, a nonprofit dedicated to the rebuilding of the Yazidi homeland in Sinjar after the destruction wrought by ISIS. And she campaigns globally to draw attention to the continued plight of the Yazidi people and the need for justice for survivors of sexual violence. Her advocacy is all the more compelling and impactful given her tragic, personal experience of the atrocities unleashed on her own people. It's also more the exception than the rule—as too often nonprofits don't put the community they serve at the heart of their work, but instead treat them as passive recipients of their programs. But Nadia's example is a stark demonstration of how compelling the voices of community representatives can be when they advocate directly to those in power.

In this chapter we'll explore why and how you should center the community your organization serves in the work.

THE CENTRALITY OF COMMUNITY

The individuals and groups served by nonprofits are variously described as beneficiaries, clients, constituents, participants, partners, and stakeholders. I generally prefer to identify them as a "community" or simply "people we serve"; however, I recognize there is no ideal descriptive term given the complexity of this relationship.

A community can be defined broadly. For example, the American Red Cross serves those "suffering in the face of emergencies" around the world. Community definitions can also be narrow, such as for the Irving Park Community Food Pantry in Chicago that serves those experiencing food insecurity in "the 60641 and 60618 ZIP codes." Or maybe your community is a mixture of both. For instance, the San Francisco Symphony "exists to inspire and serve audiences and communities throughout the Bay Area and the world through the power of musical performance."

Understanding the community you serve is central to everything your organization does. As we've seen, your mission is defined by who you serve and how. Your impact is measured by the change you help bring about for members of that community. Ensuring the community is a partner in your efforts, not just a passive recipient, has the potential to deliver much greater and more sustainable outcomes for its members. It ensures they have greater power to influence and shape programs that work for them. It brings greater buy-in and accountability and an increased chance of delivering real change.

Community is at the heart of nonprofit organizations. And yet, remarkably, until quite recently, most nonprofits saw members of their community as passive recipients of their aid, not as active participants. Nonprofits, and charities in particular, have a long history of deciding what is best for the communities they serve, with little to no input or involvement from those communities. This dynamic is reflected in the use of the term "beneficiaries" or "recipients" to describe those served, the implication being that they are not partners in efforts that directly impact them.

The top-down approach by nonprofits reaches its most extreme in the concept of the "white savior"—the white, Western development organization or individual who flies into low-income countries in Africa and elsewhere to offer "solutions," lacking any deep understanding of the problem or context. Sadly, this caricature is too often a reality. Even when engagement is not overtly exploitative, a tendency can persist (e.g., within Western research organizations) to focus on extracting information without engaging the community in follow-up advocacy and action or considering how the community members might be affected.

And this behavior doesn't just happen in low-income countries. A similar dynamic plays out in the US, the UK, Canada, and across Europe. Whenever a marginalized population is receiving support from external actors who lack sufficient understanding and consideration of the agency of those they are purportedly serving, a similarly unhealthy and often exploitative dynamic unfolds.

CASE STUDY

The Problem with "Raid and Rescue"

As the anti-slavery sector developed in the 1990s and early 2000s, many nonprofits focused their time and energy on a "raid-and-rescue" model to address sex trafficking. This typically looks like a sting operation where an individual poses as a client at a brothel thought to be trafficking children. Police follow with a raid in which assumed victims are removed and detained. After their "rescue," they might receive shelter or rehabilitation services, though they often don't.

But this model—common in the sector at the time because it was viewed as effective and lent itself to sensational news stories and emotional fundraising pleas—is problematic, for many reasons. First, it frames human trafficking as solely a criminal enterprise and relies on police to ensure the safety of vulnerable people. Blanket raids treat all people as victims and disregard any sense of personal agency.[3] Police force people to leave without their consent, often detaining sex workers who choose to be there, many of whom are also subject to violence and demands for bribes at the hands of police. For those who have been trafficked and are grateful to have been removed from their traffickers, aftercare (such as shelter and counseling) is often short-term and poor quality, and can even re-traumatize survivors. In the bigger picture, the raid-and-rescue approach is heavily focused on sex trafficking and ignores the existence of many other forms of trafficking. It denies the larger factors that are at play and fails to address root causes. Without efforts to change exploitative systems, those who are "rescued" are easily replaced with other vulnerable people. Many survivors return to the exact same economic situation as they were in before being trafficked and are at high risk of being re-exploited. The raid-and-rescue approach has been most prominently touted by large, white-run, often religiously affiliated nonprofits in the US and Europe that focus on conducting rescues in low-income countries and do little to build relationships with local communities or organizations.*

---

* Perhaps the most problematic raid-and-rescue nonprofit is Operation Underground Railroad (O.U.R.), a US anti-trafficking organization that received a lot of publicity in 2023 with the release of the film *The Sound of Freedom*, based on the story of its founder and former CEO, Tim Ballard. For a critique of the film from the perspective of survivors and anti-trafficking experts, see Aubrey Lloyd and Erin Albright, "Sound of Freedom Is Everything an Anti-trafficking Film Shouldn't Be," openDemocracy, August 10, 2023, https://www.opendemocracy.net/en/beyond -trafficking-and-slavery/sound-of-freedom-tim-ballard-operation-underground -railroad-trafficking-film-review/. For more in-depth coverage of O.U.R.'s problematic raid-and-rescue model, see Anna Merlan and Tim Marchman, "Inside a Massive Anti-Trafficking Charity's Blundering Overseas Missions," *Vice*, March 8, 2021, www.vice.com/en/article/bvxev5/inside-a-massive-anti-trafficking-charitys -blundering-overseas-missions; Anna Merlan and Tim Marchman, "A Famed Anti-Sex Trafficking Group Has a Problem With the Truth," *Vice*, December 10, 2020, https://www.vice.com/en/article/k7a3qw/a-famed-anti-sex-trafficking -group-has-a-problem-with-the-truth; Meg Conley, "Called by God," *Slate*, May 11, 2021, slate.com/human-interest/2021/05/sex-trafficking-raid-operation

For far too long, nonprofits did not take seriously the harms of this approach, even when evidence was right in front of them, including individual testimonies, research, and many newsworthy cases of abuses by police and in shelters.

When the Freedom Fund started a decade ago, we explicitly focused our approach on building partnerships with locally led grassroots organizations that take a nuanced and holistic approach to trafficking. These groups are best placed to identify and carry out anti-trafficking interventions that fit the local context and are informed by the needs of the community. While this approach may sometimes mean providing care and services for survivors identified during a police raid, it more often means building community-level awareness and resistance to exploitation, working to address root causes (like exploitative business models and a lack of economic alternatives) to ensure people are not trafficked in the first place. It also means helping survivors to navigate the justice system in order to prevent perpetrators from exploiting others. While some organizations continue to focus on a raid-and-rescue framework, the tide has changed in the sector and the majority have taken up other approaches.[4]

Over the last decade or so, in a belated but seismic shift, forward-thinking nonprofits have expanded their understanding of the role of

-underground-railroad.html; Thomas Stackpole, "The New Abolitionists," *Foreign Policy*, accessed December 10, 2022, foreignpolicy.com/2015/07/22/the-new -abolitionists-mexico-dominican-republic-human-trafficking-mormon-our/; Anna Merlan and Tim Marchman, "Tim Ballard Left Operation Underground Railroad After Investigation into Claims Made by Employees," *Vice*, July 18, 2023, https://www.vice.com/en/article/m7b3ex/tim-ballard-left-operation-underground -railroad-after-investigation-into-claims-made-by-employees.

the communities they serve, with increasing recognition of the communities' agency and the need to tangibly shift power to members of these communities so they have the resources and support to define their own trajectory.

What does this mean in practice? There are several ways nonprofits can change their relationships with communities from being top-down and one-sided to healthy and intentionally built partnerships.

START WITH YOUR STAFF AND CULTURE

Ideally, your organization is broadly representative of the community you serve. Your staff need not be drawn predominantly from members of that community, but nor should it comprise staff entirely from outside that community (as is too often the case). There is a middle ground. You should always be seeking to build a team with a wide range of expertise, including leadership expertise, fundraising experience, research and technical expertise, and deep expertise on the issues confronting your organization and sector. Community members bring personal experience of the challenges your organization exists to address, and a deep understanding of what works and what doesn't, in addition to all their other skills and attributes. People who have experienced homelessness, hunger, domestic violence, extreme forms of exploitation, and the range of other wrongs that your organization might be seeking to address bring an understanding and knowledge of the relevant issues that other staff in your organization will not possess.

But hiring those with personal experience is not always feasible, regardless of your intent. Nonprofit recruitment can be challenging at the best of times, and if you are only recruiting from the community you serve, you are probably going to significantly limit your pool of candidates. While hiring those from within or close to the communities you serve should be a priority, when you do hire staff without a personal connection to the community or issue, be sure to consider how they think and talk about the issues on which you work, as well as the potential power dynamics between staff with varying connection and experience.

You may struggle to find community members with the level of experience and qualifications you are looking for. This can become a self-perpetuating problem if you don't take steps to help them acquire the necessary expertise. At the Freedom Fund, we have started investing in survivor leadership by creating fellowships for those who have experienced slavery. We've also set up a movement-building program for survivors of slavery or for those who are from the vulnerable communities with which we work, and a fund to provide unrestricted grants to organizations led by survivors.

Regardless of the composition of your staff, building a culture that centers on the experiences and expertise of the community you serve is critically important. That's a culture of respect, curiosity, learning, and humility. It's the opposite of the savior complex, where staff believe they have all the answers and nothing to learn from those they serve.

You can support and promote this culture by ensuring you have members with personal experience on your staff, arranging visits (both ways: staff to the field, and from the community to your offices), bringing in speakers, and repeatedly reminding staff of the importance of sharing knowledge and experience.

UNDERSTAND THE DIFFERENCE IN POWER

It's all well and good to talk about serving a community and building a partnership rather than a top-down relationship, but you must not gloss over the very real differences in power that contribute to the problem in the first place. Nonprofits have long been able to get away with imposing solutions and excluding those they serve from their decision-making because they hold much of the power in those relationships. They generally have the resources, particularly funding, so desperately needed by the relevant community (hence why "beneficiaries" is so commonly used as a description), and access to decision-makers and other powerholders.

In contrast, members of the community being served usually lack direct access to these resources. They may also be suffering from significant deprivation, making them highly vulnerable. At its most extreme, this power differential enables exploitation and abuse of the community that the nonprofit is committed to supporting.

CASE STUDY

When Nonprofit Staff Abuse Their Power

Oxfam GB is one of the world's leading and most highly respected humanitarian organizations, working around the world to deliver aid and assistance to those in dire need. Following the 2010 earthquake in Haiti, a number of its staff were accused of sexually exploiting and bullying vulnerable Haitian women and girls. This led to official inquiries into these and other alleged abuses, which found widespread failings at the organization.

In response to these findings, the then Oxfam GB CEO, Dhananjayan Sriskandarajah, responded:

> We work in some of the world's highest-risk contexts, from conflict zones to places where people are struggling to survive environmental disasters. These can be places where the rule of law has broken down, and where violence and sexual violence may have become institutionalised. Those providing support, whether local people or those who arrive as part of the aid effort, can find themselves in positions of extraordinary trust and power. Our shame is that we did not do enough to prevent that power from being abused . . . At its heart, this is about power. It's about redefining the relationships we have with each other, with the partners we

work with and, most importantly, with the communities we serve. But we need to be humble and recognise that how we work is going to be just as important as what we do . . . We cannot allow our institutional culture to reflect the inequalities and abuses of power that, as an organisation, we spend so much time and effort trying to eradicate.[5]

In an ideal world, those power differentials would not exist. But they do, and ignoring them doesn't help. Rather, the best approach is to acknowledge that they exist, and then identify ways in which power can be shared with and shifted to the community you work with.

INTERVIEW

Good Intentions Are Not Enough When Working with Communities

Sophie Otiende is the CEO of the Global Fund to End Modern Slavery, a global anti-slavery fund. Before this, she helped found a survivor collective in Nairobi, Kenya. Prior to that, she worked for community-based organizations in Nairobi that focus on feminism and women's rights, children's rights, and modern slavery. Here she shares her experience of carrying out community-based anti-trafficking work, and reflects on problematic assumptions made by many NGOs when entering communities.

I have been privileged to experience shifts in my life from working as a community leader in Nairobi to my current role as the head of a global funding organization. Over the years, each role I have taken has had its fair share of lessons about the work that we do in international development. In every role I have been seen as a representative of the communities I come from. As a survivor leader from Kenya, my lived experience has always been primary in the work that I do. It has always been from this perspective that I reflect on development work done in communities.

As we work in communities, we all make certain assumptions. Some are not important, but some fundamentally shift our approach and the tools that we use. One assumption that most development organizations forget is that development work as we practice it will, in most cases, be foreign to the people we claim to serve. Yet, most of our organizations enter communities with the assumption that those communities understand what we are doing. The second assumption is that the work we are doing is right for the community. These assumptions come with the expectation that communities will accept our work and that there is no need for explaining, interpreting, or even working for buy-in from the community. I have seen how this has caused harm, primarily by excluding the very people that we claim to serve. To be a foreigner means that you speak a foreign language, you have a foreign culture, a foreign identity that is different and we should never forget that.

Another assumption we make is that just because we are helping, our power will always be used for good or rather have a positive impact in the community. We also assume that "help" is always empowering to the people we support. However, good intentions are not enough. We can still harm with good intentions. As a survivor leader, one of the things I have accepted is people's curiosity when it comes to details of my experience. The curiosity is well intended, the knowledge that we get from hearing about survivors' experiences can inspire people and ultimately lead people to act but this curiosity can be harmful. Not all survivors enjoy telling their stories and, in most cases, our experiences are not the only thing that we want remembered. Communities want to be part of the process rather than just be beneficiaries of interventions we make. The way we share power is by co-creating interventions in communities rather than coming to implement them. What we have to realize is that communities were surviving before our interventions and they will continue to survive after we leave; ensuring that our interventions go beyond the timelines that limit us, requires us to share the power we hold to them.[6]

SEEK AND ACT ON COMMUNITY FEEDBACK

Your work will be better informed and positioned to drive change if you actively seek input and feedback from the community you serve. This should be obvious, but too often nonprofits don't actively solicit contributions from those they serve for a number of reasons, including: the organization's culture may not value listening to others; leaders may assume that those implementing programs already know all there is to know; or resources may be tight, and listening to the community may be considered an unnecessary extra burden. Whatever the reason, you must continuously seek input and act on it as best you can.

This can be done in various ways—for example, by conducting surveys or focus groups of the community, setting up standing councils or other structures with community representatives, or carrying out participatory action research.

Seeking input not only improves the quality of your interventions but can build buy-in from those you serve, as it demonstrates a degree of accountability. If they understand that you seek and act upon community feedback, you will earn greater trust.

INTERVIEW

How to Include Community Perspectives in Your Work

Further observations of Sophie Otiende, CEO of the Global Fund to End Modern Slavery and Community Leader in Kenya.

What can we do to ensure that our assumptions about communities do not lead to exclusion or lead to harm? Here are a couple of key lessons:

1. We need to hire community members—this is important because they act as a bridge that we can use to get into communities and as ambassadors for our work. Local experts do not only bring knowledge of the work, they also bring lived experience, which is a lens that will ensure that we understand how our interventions will be received. Finally, hiring from the communities is not just about representation but is also one of the most effective ways to invest in those communities.

2. We need to recognize that trust is a process and it's not our right—our work relies on communities trusting us and they do not owe us that trust. Our work is paralyzed when we are not trusted, yet I rarely see organizations invest time in relationship-building in communities. Understanding that trust is a process also requires the investment of time, this is why designing long-term work in communities is better than short-term projects. The longer we have to implement interventions, the better. Long-term interventions allow us to build trust.[7]

At the Freedom Fund, our community includes those individuals in slavery or at risk of it, and the 150 frontline organizations with which we partner that work directly with those at risk of exploitation. We took too long to start surveying our partners, but now we commission an independent nonprofit consultancy to do this, seeking our partners' anonymous feedback on what we are doing well and what can be improved. The survey consists of standard questions that the consultancy has been asking for years on behalf of ninety leading international nonprofits and foundations, with more than seven thousand local partners participating during that time. This standardization allows the consultancy to benchmark organizations' results against others who have taken the survey.

Overall, our partners rated the Freedom Fund significantly above the global benchmark average on nearly all the questions. The consultancy advised that our results on some questions were the highest they had ever received, specifically on Freedom Fund's flexibility in letting partners adjust their plans mid-grant, our transparency and accountability, and our efforts to shift power to vulnerable groups. And where the results were not as positive, it provided us with a valuable opportunity to discuss with partners and find ways to address the issues they raised. Besides the valuable feedback we obtain, the fact that we do the survey is well received by our partners, and helps strengthen the relationship.*

SUPPORT COMMUNITIES TO ADVOCATE FOR THEMSELVES

Many nonprofits are professional advocates for the causes they support, with well-trained staff who lobby officials and other powerholders.

---

* For more details of these results, see Dan Vexler, "Are We Staying True to Our DNA?" Freedom Fund website, January 12, 2023, www.freedomfund.org/blog /true-to-our-dna/.

Habitat for Humanity says, "we advocate to change policies and systems so that we can eliminate barriers to adequate, affordable housing."[8] March of Dimes declares that they "lobby both Congress and the Administration and maintain strong relationships with policymakers across the political spectrum. Our priorities include a wide range of maternal child health issues."[9] To support its work on refugees, World Vision is "educating members of Congress about the refugees' realities in the region and working to maximize humanitarian aid to those in desperate need."[10]

This model of advocacy is a powerful way of driving change—but it can be even more powerful when those you are advocating for make the case themselves. A key way to shift power is to support members of the community you serve to speak on their own behalf—as we saw with Nadia Murad in the opening section of this chapter. To take another example, a refugee describing to members of Congress the perils of her journey out of Taliban-run Afghanistan to seek asylum, and what can be done to improve outcomes of the many thousands in her situation, is likely to be compelling, and far more compelling than a nonprofit staff member making the case on behalf of the refugees. Or picture a formerly homeless person advocating to city hall officials on behalf of a planning application for the shelter nonprofit that provided her refuge and options when she most needed them.

Just as importantly, the shift gives agency to that individual to tell her own story in her own voice. Such advocacy should not be conducted as a "show-and-tell," but rather to empower those most directly impacted to help shape policy decisions.

To support such advocacy, you will often need to provide advocacy training, use your relationships and networks, and bring community members to conferences and other events where they can directly access officials, funders, and other powerholders. You will need to make space and release control. And cede power.

The most important relationship your organization will have is with those it serves. They are central to your organization's purpose. But to effectively serve that community, you also need resources, particularly funding. This makes your funders another critically important partner for your organization, and we'll explore that relationship in the next chapter.

PEOPLE AND COMMUNITIES ACTION POINTS

Ensure Those You Serve Are at the Center

- Put the people and the community your organization serves at the center of your work.
- In so doing, recognize the very real differences in power between your organization and those it serves, and identify ways to help shift power to them.
- Continuously seek community feedback on your work and act on it.
- Promote those you serve by supporting them to advocate on their own behalf and helping them get access to those in power.

CHAPTER 9

Funders

Build Resonant Relationships to Encourage Giving

> *The hope you feed with your gift is likely to feed your own.*
> —MacKenzie Scott[1]

One of the more joyful experiences in my nonprofit career started with an enigmatic email, from someone I'd never heard of, with an obscure email address and domain. It read:

I support the efforts of donors who are interested in giving to Freedom Fund after learning about your work through a wide range of sources . . . I was hoping to schedule a quick ~20-minute follow-up call to discuss next steps . . . Given donor confidentiality, which I'll explain further on the call, this conversation should be just the two of us.

A hazard of being a nonprofit CEO is that I regularly receive pitches from fundraising consultants, often framed to imply donor interest in the Freedom Fund. This email was sufficiently ambiguous that I thought it might be one of those. I couldn't find any information about the sender on the internet to enlighten me one way or the other. But I was also aware that one of the world's most generous philanthropists, MacKenzie Scott, was in the process of making a round of big grants to impactful nonprofits, and that she operated with a high degree of confidentiality. So part of me hoped that this email was a prelude to a grant from her. But given how many other organizations deserved her support, I largely discounted that possibility.

I scheduled a call as requested. A week later, my heart jumped when the woman who had emailed me started our call with, "I represent MacKenzie Scott and she wants to make a significant gift to the Freedom Fund." I waited with bated breath to hear what was meant by "significant." Hearing "$35 million," I was sufficiently stunned that I asked her to repeat the amount, slowly, as I suspected I may have misheard. I hadn't. Our annual budget at this stage was $18 million. What's more, the proposed funding was completely unrestricted, meaning it was entirely up to the Freedom Fund to decide how to spend the funds. We could spend them in one year, over multiple years, or put them into an endowment. We could spend them on programs or fundraising or on our own infrastructure—such as purchasing an office building—or a mix of these. Our sole obligations were to (a) keep the news confidential until it was publicly announced by Ms. Scott, and (b) provide her team with a three- or four-page summary each year for three years on the work of our organization. That was it. The $35 million was deposited in our bank account a week later, and a public announcement was made a few weeks after that.

I hesitate to open this chapter with this story, which clearly falls at the far end of the fundraising spectrum. As such, can it hold any useful lessons for other organizations? For most small nonprofits, a $5,000 donation is a big deal, and rightly so. But I do think this experience, even though it's an outlier, is still illustrative of important elements of the fundraising process. For a start, it's not a unique experience—as of early 2023, Ms. Scott has now given away over $14 billion to over 1,600 nonprofits.[2] But the larger point is that big gifts don't just fall out of the sky. Not even this one.

Several months before this call, we had been approached by the Bridgespan Group, the world's largest philanthropic consultancy firm, operating on behalf of an anonymous donor, who had asked it to carry out due diligence on the Freedom Fund. We went through an exhaustive process with them: sharing several years' worth of accounts, board papers, detailed documentation of our impact and monitoring processes, strategic plan and operating plans, and participating in a couple of probing meetings. Again, I was conscious that Bridgespan had acted for Ms. Scott in the past, but they also acted for hundreds of other donors, so I had no way of knowing if this process would lead to any specific commitment by Ms. Scott or any other donor. After hearing nothing from the company for a couple of months after the due diligence, I'd largely given up whatever faint hope I had that this could be the prelude to a big gift.

And arguably, the process didn't even start with Bridgespan outreach. We were only in a position to attract the attention of Ms. Scott and Bridgespan, and to pass the scrutiny of such an exhaustive process, because of the quality of the organization and the impact of our work. And those were many years in the making.

THE COMPONENTS OF SUCCESSFUL FUNDRAISING

There are no shortcuts to fundraising. There are many components that go into effective fundraising, and the more of these you can draw upon, the more successful your fundraising will be. They include:

- A compelling cause
- A clear strategy
- Commitment by the leadership to fundraising efforts
- A powerful story of what you have done, and plan to do

- Demonstrated impact
- A credible team, starting with the CEO
- An ability to build relationships with potential donors
- An ability to maintain relationships with existing donors
- A record of delivering on your commitments

The mix will differ for each organization and will change during the life of a nonprofit. A start-up nonprofit won't have demonstrated impact, so its fundraising efforts will rely more on strategy and story. A well-established nonprofit will have a demonstrated history of impact, so its fundraising will likely highlight delivery, relationships, and future plans.

At the heart of all successful fundraising efforts are relationships. You need resonant relationships with your funders, particularly when raising from foundations and philanthropists. You also need a strong relationship with members of the public, or governments, if you are seeking contributions from them—though in those cases the relationships will be different, and other factors may have added weight. And the starting point for relationships is the attitude you bring to fundraising. If you don't have the right mindset, you will struggle to build the relationships you need.

LEADERS MUST EMBRACE FUNDRAISING

Your organization may have a compelling mission and strategy, outstanding staff, a track record of impact, and exciting opportunities ahead of it to drive powerful change, but if it can't mobilize the necessary funding, then it will struggle to achieve its objectives. The case for the importance of fundraising is as straightforward as that. As the leader, you are responsible for ensuring your organization gets that funding. You can do that yourself or via colleagues, but however you do it, you are ultimately responsible. You will be a much more successful fundraiser if you embrace that truth instead of having to be dragged kicking and screaming to the fundraising table.

Many CEOs feel deeply uncomfortable about fundraising, and I understand that. Some think that, given they are working on a powerful cause, the best use of their time is to focus on the issues and delivery and not on asking donors for money. But there will be no delivery if you don't have the funding you need.

Others think that asking for money is beneath them, or somehow tawdry. But until you come up with a different funding model, then to the extent that you require donors to give to your organization you will need to accept that almost all nonprofits have to ask donors for funding. Very few nonprofits generate substantial funding of their own, so most need to rely on others to provide financial support. The sooner you accept that reality, the better placed your organization will be.

For myself, I've enthusiastically embraced my fundraising role, as I see myself, as CEO, strongly placed to make the case for the impact and change that donors can support by funding the Freedom Fund. And, in turn, the more successful we are at mobilizing funding, the more ambitious we can be. I find that highly motivating.

THE IMPORTANCE OF RELATIONSHIPS

When you are asking people to give to your organization, you need to persuade them that they should support your cause and organization over others (or in addition to them). To do this effectively, you need to tell a compelling story, and you need to build a resonant relationship. Donors give to organizations that align with their values and interests, and in response to perceived needs.[3]

Then, when they become donors, you need to maintain that relationship—both to honor the giving, and to encourage their ongoing investment. The research shows that connections and a relationship with nonprofit organizations are key drivers of charitable giving.[4] As I repeatedly remind my staff, every existing donor is a potential future donor;

you want them to renew their funding when their current grant expires and to stay involved with your organization.

I take donor relationships a step further, and generally try to stay in touch with funders even when they have stopped funding our organization. I do this first because they have already provided funding to the cause I believe in, for which I remain thankful. And secondly, a former donor can always become a future donor or, if not, they can still be a powerful advocate for your work and help persuade others to support your organization.

There is no secret to building a strong relationship with a donor. It's much the same as building any resonant relationship. You need to engage them in the cause, the organization, and the change they can contribute to. You need to do your research and ensure that you understand their priorities and can make a compelling case for why they align with those of your organization. Nothing is more frustrating to a funder than someone pitching them for something completely unrelated to their known interests, without any effort to build a meaningful connection. Wearing my other hat, as a funder (as the Freedom Fund has provided financial support to some 150 grassroots organizations around the world), I often get unsolicited appeals for funding from organizations. Too often, they haven't taken the time to find out which countries or regions we work in or, sometimes, the issues we work on. This is a waste of everyone's time.

A common mistake that fundraisers make with donors, particularly with those making large gifts, is to make the relationship overtly transactional. Donors become understandably irritated being treated primarily as a checkbook and subjected to aggressive pitches on why they should donate. Of course, the relationship has a transactional element—you are asking someone to give your organization money, after all—but being treated solely in terms of their ability to give is problematic for most donors. This is why you and your organization must invest in the relationship before making any pitch. Build the relationship, engage on the cause, and then you can talk about how the funder can contribute to advancing the mission.

INTERVIEW

The Challenge of Raising Funds
for a Start-Up Nonprofit

Observations from the CEO of a start-up education charity, based in Europe, working in Africa to support educational institutions.

When I took over as CEO we had just over one year of funding and very weak prospects. Fundraising was the element I was probably most nervous about and so this is the issue that gave me the most sleepless nights. In a way I didn't realize quite how urgent the situation was, which I think was a good thing as it meant I concentrated on the things that ultimately got us back on track: clarifying our strategy and narrative and embedding a strong senior team. Panicking would have been a very bad option. At the same time I did go knocking on pretty much any door I could find and I was lucky enough to have an energetic chair who found a huge number of doors for me to knock on and knocked on quite a few himself.

Ultimately, I spent a lot of time in conversations that went nowhere but as a consequence, I am now an absolute expert on what will and won't waste my time and I think probably everyone has to go through that phase if they don't have the previous experience. But the lesson I really want to draw attention to is about holding your nerve and the importance of believing in what you do. I believed in my team and our mission and I knew what we were delivering could make a difference. I wasn't blindly optimistic, I knew this wasn't enough to succeed in fundraising, but it motivated me. Even if we had to radically downsize or shut up shop I knew that right until the last day we would be having a positive impact in the world and that wouldn't have been a waste of time. This is what allowed me not to pass my concerns onto the team beyond the senior level team and what allowed me not to panic even with them.

The other critical component was the support of my board, particularly my chair and treasurer. I never felt like I was in it alone and like good coaches, they cheered me on and helped me stay focused whenever I felt like panicking. I know several CEOs have difficult relationships with their boards and I simply don't know how they do their jobs.[5]

FUNDRAISING CAN BE TRANSFORMATIVE

I was deeply apprehensive about fundraising when I took up my role as CEO of the Freedom Fund. I had experience in leading organizations, running programs, and other key areas of leadership, but I had never had any significant direct fundraising responsibility. What if I wasn't good at it? Fundraising on an ambitious scale was defined by my board as one of my primary objectives. Specifically, our strategy called for us to raise $100 million in six years—a daunting target for any incoming CEO, let alone one of a start-up.

I had no choice but to embrace the challenge. My first step was to reframe it. I internalized that we had a powerful cause and strategy and the backing of some visionary philanthropists. That made the Freedom Fund an attractive partner to potential funders, and I decided we should be looking to build partnerships, not just donor–recipient relationships. Given that we had a donor board,* I could make a strong case to potential

---

* Boards take many shapes, as we explored in chapter seven on boards. They can comprise subject matter experts, donors, professionals (e.g., lawyers, accountants), representatives of the communities being served, and others. Some have a much more active role in fundraising than others.

donors: they had the opportunity to invest and participate in a powerful new initiative with like-minded partners, including by joining our
board. They could become a part of something bigger than themselves
and use their funding and power for good. So framed, the relationship
was less transactional and more transformative in nature—for both the
donor and the recipient.*

I soon found that I enjoyed making the case to potential funders
about why they should get involved. I got energy out of sharing with
others how their resources could help the Freedom Fund transform the
lives of some of the world's most vulnerable people. And I discovered
that singing the virtues of something you believe in deeply is not hard,
particularly when the purpose is to increase your resources to do that
work. We ended up raising over $100 million in our first five years, and
$200 million by the end of our eighth year.

Funders who embrace their role as partners generally find the experience more rewarding and engaging than those who view their role simply as providing funding and nothing more. At the Freedom Fund, most
of our big donors have become valuable, multi-year partners. Many are
represented on our board.

However, even when you are successful in your fundraising, and even
when you have a strong partnership with your donor, a significant power
imbalance usually exists between you, in favor of the donor. This is more
the case with some donors than others, but the imbalance is always there.
But steps can be taken to rebalance the dynamics, as we'll see.

---

* On transforming the donor–grantee relationship, see Jeffrey C. Walker, Jennifer
McCrea, and Karl Weber, *The Generosity Network: New Transformational Tools for
Successful Fund-Raising* (New York: Deepak Chopra Books, 2013).

REFRAME YOUR ISSUES TO APPEAL
TO DIFFERENT DONORS

You can ensure your work appeals to a broader range of donors by reframing it for different groups of donors, depending on their interests. In the Freedom Fund's case, most donors are primarily interested in supporting efforts to combat modern slavery. But others are interested in work that supports "localization"—i.e., partnerships with community-based groups and highly vulnerable populations (whether on slavery, or girls' education, or caste issues, or climate change, or some other pressing issue).* Others are more interested in our governance model, with a particular interest in "collaborative funds" where funders closely collaborate in the governance and running of the fund.† Given that our work already encompasses all of these issues and approaches, we seek to appeal to all of these funders and present our work in different ways to different funders, depending on their interests.

More in Common, the community-building organization, identified that the "social cohesion" field was relatively small for funding, but that a lack of such cohesion was blocking progress on many other issues, such as climate change. So, it developed a new stream of activity focused on applying its insights on community polarization to climate change and this quickly became its single largest source of funding.[6]

The key is to ensure you are reframing existing work that is consistent with your mission, and not embarking on new work that is not core

---

* See, for example, Daryl Grisgraber and Marin Belhoussein, "When Local Leaders Speak, We Need to Listen: USAID Puts Forward Its Vision," Oxfam website, November 9, 2022, https://politicsofpoverty.oxfamamerica.org/when-local-leaders -speak-we-need-to-listen-usaid-puts-forward-its-vision/. See also Funding Frontline Impact, www.fundingfrontlineimpact.org.

† See, for example, Alison Powell and Michael John, "Releasing the Potential of Philanthropic Collaborations," The Bridgespan Group website, December 14, 2021, https://www.bridgespan.org/insights/philanthropic-collaborations.

to your mission simply to appeal to donors, which will quickly lead to mission drift.

DEALING WITH POWER DYNAMICS AND BUILDING TRUST

Much as we might like to persuade ourselves otherwise, funders are usually more important to nonprofits than the other way around. Funders can invest in many different organizations in a sector they care about, or in different sectors entirely. Most nonprofits, on the other hand, have an ongoing struggle to expand their pool of donors. So, while the relationship certainly isn't one-way—donors get a lot out of their partnership with a successful and impactful nonprofit—the different opportunities for funders and nonprofits do create a power imbalance.

Some donors are not conscious of the power imbalance, some of them ignore it, and others are not troubled by it. Most of these donors make heavy demands of nonprofits, without much consideration of the burden this places on their grantees to service the donor, diverting resources from the mission. To take a common example, many nonprofit leaders have had the experience of spending weeks completing a detailed funding proposal in the complex format required by the donor, followed by weeks of meetings and discussions and revisions to the proposal, only to be told that the application was declined. That outcome is part of the job, and of course there's no guarantee that every funding application will be successful. But donors for their part can usually find ways to simplify the process, to reduce the time nonprofits spend on unsuccessful (and successful) applications. In fact, one of the most valuable responses a potential donor can provide is an early "no"—saving a nonprofit unnecessary time and effort.

Other donors insist on the nonprofit following the funder's priorities, which may not be what the nonprofit has identified as the most effective strategy to tackle the issue at hand. At its most egregious, this insistence can lead to serious mission drift for the nonprofit. The CEO and colleagues should always try to work with the donor to minimize the unnecessary demands, and to ensure that the funding genuinely advances the organization's mission and doesn't pull it off course. In the worst-case scenario, funding that is too onerous (i.e., too restrictive, or with disproportionate reporting restrictions) or too far off mission should be refused. At the Freedom Fund, on a number of occasions, we have reluctantly pulled out of application processes or sometimes even turned down funding opportunities that were not aligned with our strategy because they would end up being more an impediment than a benefit to our mission.

However, the funder relationship doesn't have to be like this, and for many donors, it isn't; indeed, there is a growing recognition among donors of the need for greater trust in the organizations they fund. These donors choose to constrain their power, and work with the nonprofit to provide support best geared to achieve the nonprofit's objectives. This "trust-based philanthropy" takes various forms. Done well, trust-based philanthropy helps address the inherent power imbalances between funders, nonprofits, and the communities they serve. All nonprofit leaders should be pushing for the funding they receive to be trust-based in nature, to the greatest extent possible.

MacKenzie Scott framed it well in the blog post in which she announced the gift to the Freedom Fund and 285 other nonprofits:

> People struggling against inequities deserve center stage in stories about change they are creating. This is equally—perhaps especially—true when their work is funded by wealth. Any wealth is a product of a collective effort that included them. The social structures that inflate wealth present obstacles to them. And despite those obstacles, they are providing solutions that benefit us all.
>
> Putting large donors at the center of stories on social progress is a distortion of their role. We are attempting to give away

a fortune that was enabled by systems in need of change. My team's efforts are governed by a humbling belief that it would be better if disproportionate wealth were not concentrated in a small number of hands, and that the solutions are best designed and implemented by others.[7]

WHY NONPROFITS SHOULD ENCOURAGE TRUST-BASED GIVING FROM DONORS

Trust-based giving seeks to reduce power imbalances between donors and their grantees, and can include some or all of the following elements:

Unrestricted giving enables you to decide where the funding can be most effectively deployed for the biggest impact.

Multi-year funding gives your organization the security to plan for the future and the ability to respond to urgent needs. Receiving a three- to five-year funding commitment, for example, fosters sustainability and encourages collaboration, as you can plan accordingly.

Simplified and streamlined processes. Nonprofits spend a huge amount of time on funder-driven applications and reports, many of which only get cursory attention. Ask donors to strip it back. They should start by understanding what the nonprofit tracks and measures already. Then they should work out what they really need to know, and what they can't ascertain on their own account.

Transparency and responsiveness. Donors should try not to waste a nonprofit's precious time. They should be clear about what they will and won't fund. You should encourage them to make timely decisions and be clear about how they are making them and transparent about what they don't know. You should ask them to involve you and other grantees in strategy development as much as possible.

A willingness to seek out and act on feedback. You should encourage donors to survey those they fund—if they are willing to genuinely listen to the feedback. In doing so, they need to be conscious of how much time they are asking of you and other grantees and offer compensation if it's a significant amount of time, as they would a consultant.

Support beyond the check. Some donors offer support in addition to funding, e.g., communications support, leadership coaching, or other forms of support. One of the most effective ways donors can support your organization is by introducing you to other donors in their network. The power of peer donor validation can be an effective way to build relationships with new donors.

THE POWER OF GOOD STORYTELLING

How do you go about making the case for investment in your sector and organization? One of the most effective ways is to tell an engaging story. Nonprofits have the advantage of having a compelling cause to advocate for. The research shows that storytelling is a powerful fundraising tool.[8]

As a leader, you are the main spokesperson for your organization, though you shouldn't be the only one. Other staff, particularly the individuals closest to those you serve, are well placed to talk compellingly about your work, as are those you serve (provided it's not done in an exploitative way). But often, the expectation of donors, or conference organizers, will be for the CEO to be the front person telling the story about your organization's work.

Many people are not comfortable with public speaking, or even in putting together a story about their work. But it's an important skill, so if you are one of those people, you need to invest in developing your public-speaking and storytelling skills.

CASE STUDY

A Framework for Powerful Storytelling

When it comes to storytelling, I often draw on a framework developed by renowned community organizer Dr. Marshall Ganz. His first activism was with the Freedom Riders in the '60s, supporting the enrollment of African American voters in the American South. Then he worked with legendary activist Cesar Chavez mobilizing farm workers in California to fight for more humane labor conditions. After returning to Harvard, Ganz completed his PhD in sociology and developed his three-part public narrative framework: the story of **self**, the story of **us**, and the story of **now**. In Marshall's words:

> A leadership story is first a story of self, a story of why I've been called. Some people say, "I don't want to talk about myself," but if you don't interpret to others your calling and your reason for doing what you're doing, do you think it will just stay uninterpreted? No. Other people will interpret it for you. You don't have any choice if you want to be a leader. You have to claim authorship of your story and learn to tell it to others so they can understand the values that move you to act, because it might move them to act as well.
>
> The second part, the story of us, is the answer to the question of why should we, the audience, engage.

Why does it matter to our community? Why should we take action? . . .

And the final part, the story of now, is the answer to why should we act NOW? It speaks to the realization that there is a problem out there that we as a community need to address, and the time to act is now. It's a way of trying to bring balance between the problem we now perceive and our power to help address it.[9]

There is a narrative arc to a story told in this way. Over some years now of doing this, I've found that people want to know why they should listen to me—e.g., why I care about the cause, my experiences of meeting survivors and perpetrators (story of self), why they should engage with our cause—e.g., how trafficking, and especially forced labor, touches all of us through goods we consume, and our common humanity (story of us), and why they should take action now—e.g., to end horrendous and conscience shocking abuses taking place as we speak (story of now). Applying this framework to any cause you believe in will help you paint a compelling picture as to why your audience needs to engage and act.

Introducing your audience to the reality of an issue you are working on is another effective way to tell a story. You can use blogs, videos, photos, and social media. Producing a video can require a significant investment of resources, but that has to be weighed against the return. A well-designed video can last the organization for years and be used on the website as well as for events and presentations—so it can be an investment well worth making.

Site visits are also a highly effective way to expose donors to your work, giving them the opportunity to meet those your nonprofit serves.

For donors and others to see firsthand what your organization does can be transformational. That's why the big humanitarian charities organize for donors and celebrities to travel to the countries they work in. But these trips carry risks and need to be done respectfully and sensitively, so as not to become "poverty porn" where the donor or other guests are flown in to see community members perform on demand[10]—that's the worst reinforcement of damaging power dynamics. The visits should be as unobtrusive as possible. It's vital that community members understand the reasons for the visits and parameters. Permission should be obtained before photographs are taken, and safeguarding measures strictly complied with. Done well, site visits offer a deeper understanding of the work your organization does and can be hugely persuasive with potential donors, bringing them face-to-face with the reality of the cause. Site visits should be in your armament of fundraising tools but handled with care and respect.

COMPETITION FOR FUNDING

A perpetual lament for nonprofits is the lack of available funding. That has always been, and will remain, the case. However, the claim is also worth interrogating. Usually, what is meant is: not enough funding exists for the individual nonprofit or for the sector. But neither of these are constants.

For a start, the scale of actual and potential philanthropic funding is huge. According to Giving USA's annual report on nonprofit donations, US charitable giving in 2021 totaled $485 billion,[11] a 4 percent increase since 2020. These numbers are difficult to comprehend. That said, most philanthropic funding is directed to large institutions—the majority of philanthropic giving goes to churches, universities, hospitals, and museums. In contrast, most nonprofits remain small—92 percent of US nonprofits spend less than $1 million annually, and 75 percent spend less than $100,000.[12]

In order to access a significant share of the available funding, your organization needs to make the case that it's an effective vehicle for donor investment. The challenge in doing this is that you are often implicitly (or sometimes explicitly) comparing your performance against your peers. That's not ideal. But, on the other hand, to the extent that resources are limited, and if you believe your organization has a compelling purpose and strategy, then you must mobilize the resources you need, even if that means differentiating yourself from peers.

SAYING NO TO FUNDERS

Just as important as raising funding is knowing when to say no. Many leaders struggle with this, understandably. After all the effort you and your team put into mobilizing funding, turning down a donor can be very hard.

But you might need to do so. For example, if the funding comes with demands attached that may drag you significantly off mission. Or funding that may be unduly demanding of your time and resources. For example, if you are a large or midsized nonprofit, then filling in a forty-page proposal and going through multiple rounds of interviews for a $20,000 grant (which comes with its own onerous reporting requirements) may not be worth your time and effort.

Another example involves potential reputational risks. This occurs most commonly with corporate donors or controversial philanthropists. A stark example is that of the Sackler family in the US. For decades they have been generous funders of art galleries and museums in the US and Europe, usually requiring the family name to be prominently displayed on halls, wings, or whole buildings. As awareness has grown of the family's role as owners and directors of the company largely responsible for the OxyContin drug crisis across the US, recipient organizations have been scrambling to sever all ties.[13]

Corporate donations can be problematic for many nonprofits. Some nonprofits, particularly human rights ones, such as Human Rights Watch and Global Witness, don't take any corporate funding. For others, corporate funding is an important and legitimate source, within bounds. The situation becomes problematic when the association with the company undermines the nonprofit's credibility or integrity.* Turning to art galleries and museums again (their public profile makes them attractive to donors and protesters alike), these are often targeted by climate campaigners for accepting sponsorship from oil and gas companies.[14]

Sometimes corporate donors are investing (in part or whole) to burnish their reputations by association with a worthy cause. There's nothing necessarily wrong with that, but the more problematic the corporation's reputation, the more generous it may be as a funder—and the more challenging for a nonprofit to balance needed funds over reputational risk.

Good due diligence is important, as is a thoughtful policy on donors. But these don't really help with the borderline cases. With those cases, you need to compare potential reputational risk with the benefit to be gained from the funding. You can perhaps reduce the risks by insisting on the funding being unrestricted—showing support for the organization's mission as a whole—as opposed to being restricted to a particular program the funder wants to highlight. A willingness to provide core funding can demonstrate good intent by the donor. And obviously the corporate donor should have no ongoing say on how you implement your programs.

In the end, as with many other decisions, you need to weigh the wider interests of your cause and mission, apply your values, and consult widely. You can look to the behavior of peer organizations. Which other nonprofits are funded by the corporations in question and what are their considerations? You can engage your board, and definitely should if there is real potential for reputational risk.

---

* For example: Rachel Millard, "Save the Children Rejects $1M Ukraine Donation from North Sea Oil Company," *Daily Telegraph*, March 22, 2022, https://www.telegraph.co.uk/business/2022/03/22/save-children-rejects-1m-ukraine-donation-north-sea-oil-company/.

CASE STUDY

Establishing a Policy on the Funding That Your Nonprofit Will Accept

FRIDA is a nonprofit that aims to "provide young feminist organizers with the resources they need to amplify their voices and bring attention to the social justice issues they care about." This support takes the form of grants as well as opportunities for learning, convening, and movement building. As a feminist organization focused on helping activists to upend unequal power structures, FRIDA acknowledges the inherent tension between the traditional philanthropic sector, which exists in large part because of inequalities it opposes, and the organization's need to fundraise in order to have greater impact. In order to adhere to its values, FRIDA has created a "resource mobilization ethics policy"[15] that it uses to maintain transparency and discipline around fundraising and set boundaries around the types of money the organization is willing to accept. It was developed through consultation with FRIDA staff, board, advisers, grantee partners, activists, and peer organizations.

The policy sets out FRIDA's approach to fundraising and its processes for making decisions about whether to accept a gift. It specifies which staff can make decisions about gifts and establishes a Resource Mobilization Taskforce, which includes staff, advisers, and grantees and meets periodically to review questions about specific donors. It describes the type of donors FRIDA hopes to work with: donors who align with its values, are open to learning, and recognize their own wealth and privilege. It also sets out a list of "non-negotiables"—donor traits or activities that FRIDA would never accept funding from. These are largely focused on donor activities that could compromise FRIDA's or its grantee partners' work, that go directly against FRIDA's mission and values, or that are actively and directly doing harm to people or the environment. FRIDA also lays out its intention to positively influence donor behavior, acknowledging that a decision sometimes needs to be made about whether engagement with a "less-than-perfect" donor might be worthwhile. It sets forth a set of questions to guide these discussions.

THE POWER OF PUBLIC GIVING

I don't want to end this chapter talking about reputational risk. Fundraising can and should be more uplifting than that. I'm also conscious that in this chapter I've focused mainly on giving by philanthropists and governments, over giving from members of the public. So let me share a story about the power of public giving, very different from the story I opened this chapter with. While the opening story was about one of my joyful nonprofit experiences, this one is about one of my most moving experiences, in deeply distressing circumstances.

When the British MP Jo Cox was brutally murdered, there was an overwhelming outpouring of public grief and anger in the UK. Members of the public sought out ways to honor Jo and all she had stood for and to support her young family. I joined with a small group of Jo's friends to set up an online fundraising page for those who wanted to contribute. Her husband, Brendan, decided that none of the money would go to the family. Instead, the funding would be directed to three causes "closest to her heart," to support her legacy. The first cause was the White Helmets, a courageous volunteer organization providing emergency search and rescue and medical evacuation for civilians under attack in cities in Syria. The second was Hope not Hate, which campaigns against racism and extremism in the UK. The third was Royal Voluntary Service, which provides voluntary services for the elderly across the UK, including in Jo's constituency.

We expected to raise perhaps tens of thousands of dollars for these worthy causes. But within a day, members of the public had donated over £500,000 ($700,000). Within a month the effort raised £1.5m ($2.1 million), and almost £2 million ($2.8 million) by the time we closed it a couple of months later. More than 46,000 people made donations. This comment from one donor was representative of many: "I didn't know her but it is obvious that she touched so many people in many parts of the world. We have lost a huge talent, a truly genuine and caring human being. I hope everyone can continue with her philosophy of love and not hatred. RIP Jo." Another said, "[I] pray your family gets comfort in this dark hour. I am an immigrant, who found hope in your words of tolerance, compassion and love; in a world where we are written off by many as evil invaders, benefits scoundrels, rapists and terrorists."[16]

We distributed £500,000 to each of the three causes, and the balance was used to launch the Jo Cox Foundation to advance Jo's legacy and support a range of issues she deeply cared about—an effort that continues to this day.

FUNDER ACTION POINTS

Build Resonant Relationships to Encourage Giving

- Be at the forefront of fundraising efforts for your nonprofit.
- Align funders to your cause through resonant relationships.
- Understand the difference in power between funders and grantees, and work to build a more equal, trust-based relationship.
- Be prepared to turn down funding if it will pull you off mission, or come with unacceptable conditions or risks.

CHAPTER 10

Peer Organizations and Networks

Collaborate to Scale Impact

> *I would unite with anybody to do right and with nobody to do wrong.*
>
> —Frederick Douglass[1]

The challenges nonprofits take on are among the toughest that societies face—hunger, disease, climate change, armed conflict, racial injustice, gender inequality, and human rights abuses, to list just a few. With almost all of these challenges, a single nonprofit, no matter how effective it is, can achieve only so much on its own. But by bringing others together in support of your cause, you can accomplish significantly greater change.

A compelling example of this is Girls Not Brides, the global partnership to end child marriage. I had the honor of serving on the organization's board for a number of years and got a firsthand look at the power of its collaborative model.

"Child marriage" is too innocuous a term for a practice that ensnares an estimated twelve million girls under the age of eighteen around the world every year.[2] One in eight girls in developing countries is married under the age of fifteen.[3] This practice condemns millions of girls every year to lives of increased suffering, discrimination, and violence. It forces them to drop out of school. It traps girls and their families in a cycle of poverty. It increases rates of maternal mortality—when girls become pregnant before their bodies are ready, they are at high risk of complications during pregnancy and childbirth, which endanger the life of both mother and child. And it is a big obstacle to gender equality and the unleashing of women's potential to contribute to society.*

Yet at the beginning of the last decade, this issue was receiving scant international attention, despite the fact that nearly 40 percent of girls in the world's poorest countries are married as children, impacting some 650 million women.[4] An organization founded by Nelson Mandela decided to change this. The organization, the Elders, has eminent global figures as its past and present leaders, including Nobel Peace Prize laureates Desmond Tutu, Ellen Johnson Sirleaf, Kofi Annan, and Jimmy Carter. Its CEO at the time, Mabel van Oranje, identified child marriage as a pressing global human rights issue receiving far too little attention, and one that high-profile leaders could shine a spotlight on. The Elders agreed and launched the Girls Not Brides campaign in 2011. In 2013, the campaign became a nonprofit organization under Mabel's leadership.

Girls Not Brides's model is explicitly collaborative. It is a genuinely global partnership. Nonprofits around the world with a commitment to end child marriage can join the partnership, which, at the time of writing, included more than 1,600 member nonprofits from over one hundred countries.[5] Mabel describes its philosophy this way: "When working to end child marriage, we can all make a difference, but nobody

---

* For example, "5 Reasons Why Child Marriage Affects Us All," Camfed website, December 17, 2017, camfed.org/5-reasons-why-child-marriage-affects-us-all.

can do it alone. By working together, we can have more impact than the sum of the parts."[6]

Girls Not Brides operates as a "backbone" organization, providing its partners with research and learning resources on child marriage. It amplifies the voices of girls at risk of child marriage. It helps set up country-level partnerships to support partners to advance their own efforts and advocacy to their governments. It elevates the issue of child marriage to the highest global levels and helps generate funding and other resources for the cause.

The efforts of Girls Not Brides and its many hundreds of partners have been transformative for the issue of child marriage, which now gets much greater attention and action from international organizations like the UN, and from governments around the world. The partnership's growing profile and influence were recently highlighted when three of the world's leading philanthropists and activists for gender equity, Michelle Obama, Melinda French Gates, and Amal Clooney, launched the "Get Her There" campaign to end child marriage and "support transformative organizations such as . . . Girls Not Brides."[7] The campaign will further accelerate mobilization of resources and attention being devoted to ending child marriage.

WHY COLLABORATE?

The power of nonprofit collaboration can best be seen by comparing what success looks like for a business to that for a nonprofit. Peak success for a business usually means dominating its chosen market and marginalizing (or absorbing) the competition, so that it can generate ever greater profits, and hence maximize its financial returns. Think Microsoft or Amazon.

For a nonprofit, success is about advancing the purpose for which it exists and achieving significant impact. Achieving that impact is (or should be) more important than your organization's specific role in making it happen, or the attention it receives for doing so. For example, if your purpose is to reduce homelessness or food insecurity in a particular city, you'll presumably celebrate if that is achieved, regardless of how prominent your nonprofit was in delivering that outcome.

Effective nonprofit leaders understand this. They know there is only so much their organizations can achieve on their own. There are very real obstacles to nonprofits aggressively scaling the size and reach of their organization. For a start, unlike businesses, nonprofits rarely generate their own income. Scaling a nonprofit requires them to secure more donations and other forms of income. That, in turn, usually requires them to spend a greater proportion of their income on fundraising (as they pursue more difficult-to-obtain funding or more challenging funders or smaller service contracts), reducing the percentage available for their programs.

Given these obstacles, nonprofits should think of scale in terms of impact, not just organization size. And they should look to scale impact through collaboration and systems change rather than organization growth alone. You can grow your impact by mobilizing and influencing others to work to the same ends. Bringing together powerful coalitions, building movements, creating networks and federated structures, and advocating collectively are all ways to scale impact. If your goal is social change, you'll be much more likely to achieve it if lots of people and organizations are aligned with you and pulling in the same direction than if you proceed alone.

Of course, building networks or coalitions can be hard, as it requires agreement around shared goals and/or tactics. Reaching agreement can often require surrendering a significant degree of control or agreeing to do something differently, and leaders—especially those who are very set in their visions—can struggle with that. So, let's look at some of the ways collaboration can be achieved through networks. First, some terminology. I'm using "coalition" and "network" interchangeably here, to refer to groups of organizations coming together around a common cause or issue. These groupings can be more or less formal. Another commonly used term is "movement," though a movement is usually broader and more organic in scope, inclusive of a wider range of constituents, including networks, individuals, organizations, and other groups. Tremendously important for social change, movements are largely beyond the scope of this chapter, so we'll focus on networks and coalitions.

IDENTIFY SHARED INTERESTS

To build a network, you need a group of organizations to agree to work on a common issue. You may be dedicated to similar causes, or you may have completely different causes or ideologies but shared short- or medium-term interests. The key is to get agreement on specific things you want to do together. For example, in the modern slavery space, many groups regard all sex work as highly exploitative (even if it's done consensually by an adult) and hence seek to legally abolish the commercial sex industry. Other groups think if adults chose to engage in sex work, their choice is valid and they should receive protections just like workers in any other industry. These are fundamentally different stances. But all these groups are united in their belief that anyone who is forced or coerced into the sex industry, or under the age of eighteen, is experiencing human trafficking and should be helped to get out of that situation. When these groups unify around this shorter-term interest in supporting survivors to exit trafficking situations, they find plenty of opportunities to collaborate.

Or you may have shared endpoints but fundamentally different approaches to achieving them. The challenge here is to find common ground on issues that advance your collective objectives and leverage one another's strengths to get there.

All of this will be easier if the groups trying to collaborate share similar philosophies and approaches, but it doesn't need to be so. In fact, some of the most powerful coalitions are those that bring together organizations with fundamentally different philosophies around a shared issue. The child sex trafficking case is one example. US prison reform is another.

CASE STUDY

Unlikely Allies Come Together to Push for Criminal Justice Reform

The Coalition for Public Safety is an effort to reform the US criminal justice system that relies on collaboration across ideologies. In its own words, "In an unprecedented way, we bring together the nation's most prominent conservative and progressive organizations to pursue an aggressive criminal justice reform effort."[8] Its members include conservative groups like Americans for Tax Reform, Freedom-Works, Faith and Freedom Coalition, and Right On Crime, and more progressive ones such as the American Civil Liberties Union, the Center for American Progress, and the Leadership Conference on Civil and Human Rights. Its funders include both Koch Industries and the Ford Foundation, which generally sit on opposing ends of the ideological spectrum.

Although these groups have very different politics, they have all come to a shared conclusion: "that America's pattern of mass incarceration is bad for the country, terrible for communities, and devastating for individuals,"[9] and that it needs fixing. These groups have enough of a shared commitment to making the criminal justice system "smarter, fairer and more cost-effective"[10] that they have put aside long-standing differences to collaborate on this particular issue and have achieved significant progress as a result.

Truly powerful collaborations go beyond just having shared interests to develop a shared vision and strategy. They identify and implement shared activities. Some go further still and establish shared measurement practices and advocacy efforts. Robust coalitions often have a "backbone" or "quarterback" organization leading on much of these mechanics of collaboration—a group that is providing technical expertise to a range of groups, channeling funding or acting as a convenor for social movement leaders. Girls Not Brides and Crisis Action (see below) are both backbone organizations. Some are entirely focused on acting as a backbone, while for others, it's just one part of their identity. Typically, backbone organizations have a few major roles: guiding vision and strategy, supporting aligned activities, establishing shared measurement practices, building public will, and mobilizing funding.[11] One of the advantages of a backbone organization is that it helps overcome much of the friction impeding effective collaboration.

Regardless of your approach, collaboration requires leaders to keep their egos in check. It requires a willingness to focus on the cause over the organization's or leader's shorter-term interests around control and profile. Given that all organizations have differing objectives and approaches, to a greater or smaller degree, you won't be able to build successful coalitions if you insist on everything being done your way. Saying "you must collaborate entirely on my terms" (as happens surprisingly often) is an oxymoron. I'm often reminded of President Truman's aphorism "It is amazing what you can accomplish if you do not care who gets the credit." However, this can be hard for nonprofit leaders to accept, as, at the same time as collaborating, they are often also seeking to raise their organization's profile, demonstrate their impact, and impress donors. Most donors expect the groups they fund to be able to attribute direct impact of their funding, and true collaboration necessitates a willingness to accept complexity and nuance regarding attribution.

All the challenges aside, the time and effort invested in building effective networks—whether on an issue-by-issue basis or on a more long-standing footing—will almost always deliver greater progress on your cause than working in isolation.

CASE STUDY

Operating Behind the Scenes to Build Coalitions to Tackle Armed Conflicts

Nonprofits often seek publicity for their work—media coverage, name recognition, a strong social media presence. These can be effective ways to highlight impact and mobilize others, including funders, to their cause. So how did a nonprofit that consciously avoids publicity and deliberately operates behind the scenes become one of the most impactful conflict prevention organizations of recent decades?

I'm talking about Crisis Action,* a small, highly effective nonprofit, whose board I chaired from 2006 to 2013. It describes itself as "a catalyst and coordinator for organizations working together to protect civilians from armed conflict." Despite playing a key role in mobilizing impactful coalitions to campaign against conflicts in countries ranging from Myanmar to Yemen to Ukraine, Crisis Action is not a household name. That is by design. The organization sees its role as one to bring together and promote those coalitions and campaigns, and it can do that much more effectively by avoiding the spotlight and directing it onto others.

Crisis Action's efforts to prevent a potential genocide in the Central African Republic (CAR) illustrate the power of this approach. Following a coup early in 2013, horrific ethnic cleansing spread rapidly throughout CAR, with mass

---

* Not to be mistaken with International Crisis Group, a different and much more public conflict-prevention organization.

atrocities committed by both Muslim and Christian groups. By March, 90 percent of the capital's Muslim population had been forced from their homes or murdered. Local authorities had no ability to stop the killings. The atrocities prompted calls for international action to prevent a possible genocide.

Crisis Action, working closely with its human rights and humanitarian partners in the country, determined that, without a UN peacekeeping force, the loss of human life would be catastrophic. So it began to ring alarm bells with the United Nations and the African Union, and in Washington, DC, and European capitals. At the same time, it brought together a powerful interfaith delegation consisting of CAR's most influential Christian and Muslim leaders.

Crisis Action helped this delegation get access to the international media, including CNN, *Time* magazine, the *Washington Post*, and other outlets, while shunning media coverage for its own efforts. It also helped the delegation secure meetings with UN Secretary-General Ban Ki-moon, French President François Hollande, and all fifteen Security Council ambassadors.

These efforts proved effective. Over the course of the next few months, the African Union, the United Nations, and the European Union deployed peacekeepers to CAR. The feared genocide didn't happen, and the violence subsided.

Later, the French foreign minister commented: "Crisis Action offered the CAR religious leaders an international platform at a critical time when their calls for peace needed to be heard. Crisis Action's collaboration with the faith leaders was of enormous support to the French government's engagement in CAR."[12]

SHARE KNOWLEDGE AND EXPERTISE

Whether or not your organization is actively collaborating in a network, it can support other organizations by sharing relevant knowledge and expertise. Some organizations go further and provide training or support to peer organizations. Do this well and your nonprofit can facilitate cost-sharing and benefit the field as a whole. You can also potentially influence the thinking and strategies of the groups you help to educate, as well as the broader field.

We've pursued this approach from the earliest days of the Freedom Fund. We commission a lot of research and publish it all. We also publish a monthly bulletin of others' key research developments across the field, so that all can benefit from this knowledge. In this spirit, we have also developed an online, publicly accessible resource containing all of our templates and systems for identifying, working with, funding, and evaluating grassroots NGOs. Our objective is to encourage funders to directly support grassroots organizations, and to provide them with the tools and templates to do so. Beyond this, we recognize that many other organizations with fewer resources will benefit from understanding our approach and learnings.*

Some organizations go even further and provide funding to their peer organizations. They understand that this is a powerful way of shifting power and investing in collaborations. The Freedom Fund currently makes grants to over one hundred partner organizations. We have introduced new funding mechanisms, including a fund that provides unrestricted grants to survivor-led organizations and small grants to support inclusive convenings, in order to fill gaps that we've observed in the anti-trafficking movement.

Support does not need to be financial. Organizations can invest in coalitions by hosting others on their premises, sharing expertise or

---

* The initiative is called Funding Frontline Impact, and all the materials are available at www.fundingfrontlineimpact.org.

insider knowledge, or paying for partner staff from smaller organizations to attend convenings or participate in advocacy meetings. These modest investments can have an outsized impact in strengthening relationships.

OBSTACLES

Effective collaboration is difficult. None of the challenges are insurmountable, although, on occasion, the cost of overcoming obstacles may outweigh the benefits of collaboration. The calculation needs to be made on a case-by-case basis.

Almost invariably, one of the greatest perceived obstacles to better nonprofit collaboration is competition for funding and attention. Given nonprofits are often seeking funding from similar sources, they often hesitate to collaborate with their "competitors." In my experience, this is generally a shortsighted perspective by nonprofits and one that is rarely welcomed by philanthropists. Effective collaboration can and should grow the funding pie, as it should make you better able to demonstrate progress and impact to donors. Second, donors rarely welcome cutthroat competition for their funding and are apt to look more kindly on organizations that are explicitly collaborative in nature. Collaboration also reduces the pressure on donors to pick a "winner" out of many worthy organizations.

Another common challenge is that, in an effort to build consensus, objectives become so watered down as to be meaningless. For example, if you are advocating to a legislator, you will usually be most effective if you have a clear ask, such as voting in support of a piece of legislation. But if you go to a policymaker simply telling them they need to "do something, urgently" without specifying what—perhaps because your coalition has not been able to agree on what to ask for—then you'll be markedly less effective.

THE IMPORTANCE OF A CLEAR "ASK"

When Gareth Evans, my former boss at International Crisis Group, was foreign minister of Australia, he would often meet with human rights organizations who wanted to lobby him to act in response to an unfolding regional tragedy. In his recounting, they would come and tell him there was a pressing emergency, and he would agree. They would tell him the Australian government needed to do something and he would signal openness to action. But when he asked specifically what they wanted the government to do, more often than not they would say that was for the government to decide, not for them to recommend—likely because they hadn't agreed upon a clear ask among themselves. As Gareth pointed out, this was a hugely wasted opportunity to advocate for a clear course of action to a receptive interlocutor.

Crisis Action identifies its advocacy "asks" by engaging with all its members to identify robust policy positions that have broad (though usually not uniform) support, and then gives members the option to sign on or pass, effectively creating a coalition of the willing behind a more robust policy position. Part of being a willing collaborator is accepting that not all partners will line up on every ask or campaign, and understanding that they have their own internal stances, dynamics, and priorities to manage.

Another challenge is that many leaders, and their boards, will be more focused on the growth of their organization and its revenue than on impact—especially impact that can't be directly attributed to their organization. While this is not surprising, it's a limited perspective and will often be counterproductive over the longer term in regard to foregone relationships and perceptions in the field.

Donors can also be impediments. While many enthusiastically support the idea of nonprofit collaboration, they often don't design their funding practices to support it. For example, restricted funding and overly interventionist engagement actively undermine collaboration. On the other hand, donors can give a huge boost to collaboration by structuring their funding to supporting networks, backbone organizations, and sharing of resources.

Any nonprofit leader truly dedicated to the purpose of their organization will be focused on achieving the greatest possible impact over shorter-term organizational imperatives. However, the happy reality is that, in most cases, the two are mutually reinforcing, not in conflict. Generosity is generative in the nonprofit space, and effort spent trying to collaborate effectively with peers will usually bear dividends for the cause and your organization.

———————

This concludes the section on partners. I hope these chapters have helped explain the centrality of your partners to everything your organization does. Effective nonprofit leaders embrace this reality. They put the people and communities they serve at the center of everything they do. They build resonant relationships with their funders to fuel their work, and they collaborate with other organizations to scale impact. Done well, working closely with your partners significantly increases the chances of your organization having an outsized impact in pursuit of its purpose.

PEER ORGANIZATIONS AND NETWORKS ACTION POINTS

Collaborate to Scale Impact

- Recognize that collaboration can be a highly effective way to scale impact.
- Identify shared interests or outcomes that peer organizations can coalesce around.
- Share credit (and resources if you can) to increase the chances of collaboration succeeding.
- Don't settle for a lowest common denominator approach to collaboration. Rather, build consensus around a credible ask or strategy.

CONCLUSION

A s I was in the final stages of writing this book, I returned to the place where my nonprofit journey began. It was a scorching summer's day in the port of Fremantle, Western Australia. The sail training ship *Leeuwin* was tied up alongside "B-Shed" wharf—at the same berth I had first laid eyes on it more than thirty years before. Young crew members were ambling around the decks and one or two scampered up the rigging, wearing their blue canvas smocks and harnesses. I reminisced about some of the experiences I'd shared on that ship decades ago, from furling furiously billowing sails in howling gales to diving over the side into crystal clear ocean waters while at anchor. I reflected on how many young lives had been transformed over the decades through the opportunity to bond as makeshift teams in an unfamiliar environment while testing themselves against the elements.

I reflected, too, on the long and winding journey my career had taken since then and the many inspirational nonprofits I had worked for and with. Between them, they have spanned the globe and committed themselves to issues as diverse as armed conflict, modern slavery, child marriage, climate change, national security, and legal aid and poverty. In addition to everything else, the organizations I've been part of provide a snapshot of the huge diversity of nonprofits out there seeking to make the world a better place.

All of these nonprofits have a deep commitment to driving ambitious change. But even the most successful of them have only a fraction of the financial resources available to big corporate and government agencies. Lacking financial firepower, they have to rely on the power of their purpose and their ability to mobilize others, starting with their staff, around their vision for change. They have had to identify smart ways to change systems and collaborate to scale impact. They have been at the forefront of changing the world into an immeasurably better place in the nearly eighty years since the end of the last world war. And that's despite the dire situation we find ourselves in today with the unfolding climate emergency; war in Ukraine, Gaza, Sudan, and elsewhere; mass migration on a scale never seen before; and a host of other pressing challenges. Think of those who have been in the vanguard of efforts to sound the alarm on climate over the last few decades; of movements against conflict and the dangers of authoritarianism; and of campaigns to support refugees and address the systemic factors that cause them to flee their homelands. Invariably they are nonprofits and nonprofit leaders.

Investing in the leadership of nonprofits is about investing in efforts to make the world a better place. To describe what good leadership looks like is straightforward enough—not that writing this book has been easy. It's been a real challenge for me to distill what I've learned—from my experiences and those of others, as well as from the research—into something digestible, practical, and (hopefully) useful. I've struggled somewhat with sharing my own stories, particularly my missteps. But, all that said, the attributes of good nonprofit leadership are pretty clear. The real challenge for any leader is to actually internalize and apply them consistently.

The best nonprofit leaders I've encountered are those who combine a laser-like focus on their organization's purpose and impact with humility about their own leadership. They know they always have more to learn from their peers and those they lead. They try to avoid raw exercises of authority over colleagues in favor of bringing them along on a journey. They invest heavily in teams and culture. They model the behaviors they want to see and create space for colleagues to take risks. And they always put the people and communities they serve at the very heart of the mission. This all takes a lot of work—in fact, in my case, it's fair to say that it's the work of a lifetime. But I can't think of anything more rewarding.

ACKNOWLEDGMENTS

was fortunate enough to get a sabbatical over the summer of 2022, and this gave me the time and the space to start reflecting and writing. I very much doubt this book would have happened without that time away from work, so my first thanks go to the then board members of the Freedom Fund for providing me with the opportunity, and for much more besides: Natasha Dolby, Andrew Doust, Grace Forrest, Molly Gochman, Felicity Gooding, Alan McCormick, Mahendra Pandey, and Philippe Sion. I want to give a particular shout-out to Alan, who was the hugely influential chair of the Freedom Fund for its first decade. I'm profoundly thankful for his support and wise guidance throughout our journey together. The Freedom Fund and I owe much to him. We also owe deep thanks to Molly for her willingness to succeed Alan as chair when he stepped down.

It's daunting embarking on the writing journey, particularly as a first-time author. The experience was made considerably more enjoyable thanks to my dear friend Natasha Stott Despoja giving me the run of her family's holiday house in Provence for the first weeks of my sabbatical, for which I'm most grateful.

It proved to be a particularly productive sabbatical. Not only did I make significant progress with the research and writing, but I also proposed to my partner, Sarah Le Mesurier. To my delight, she accepted, and as a result, we now have a wonderful, blended family, bringing together my daughters, Elza and Zoya, and Sarah's, Cicely and Darcey. Sarah has impressive leadership experience herself, and I've hugely valued her wise counsel and thoughtful feedback throughout this process. She's also brought much additional joy to my life, and I love her dearly. This book is dedicated to her, now my wife, and our four wonderful daughters.

Speaking of family, my parents, Richard and Monika, and my brother, Andrew, have all been exemplars of leadership through public service all their lives, and have all inspired me in ways large and small—which I far too rarely acknowledge, but hope to make up for that somewhat by doing so here.

In doing research for this book, I reached out to a number of non-profit leaders I admire to seek their feedback on the challenges and joys of leadership. I'm grateful they took time out of their busy schedules to provide such rich and thoughtful answers to my questions. It also gave me a lot of comfort to see that so many of the issues I grapple with as a leader were highlighted in their responses and feedback. So my thanks to Catherine Chen (Polaris), Mike Davis (Global Witness), Comfort Ero (International Crisis Group), Lucy Heady (Education Sub-Saharan Africa), Mathieu Lefevre (More in Common), Françoise Moudouthe (African Women's Development Fund), Sophie Otiende (Global Fund to End Modern Slavery), Ken Roth (Human Rights Watch), Asif Shaikh (Jan Sahas), Dina Sherif (the Legatum Center at MIT), Andrew Wallis (Unseen), and Gilles Yabi (West Africa Citizen Think Tank).

I've flagged in this book the importance of having peers with whom you can share and discuss leadership challenges. In addition to those listed above, I've been most fortunate over the years to be able to draw on the wisdom and companionship of a wide group of friends, all of whom happen to be outstanding nonprofit leaders and/or board members. My gratitude to Ellen Agler (The END Fund), Caitlin Baron (Luminos Fund), Tom Brookes (Global Strategic Communications Council), Brandee Butler (Fund for Global Human Rights), Brendan Cox (Together Coalition), Tim Dixon (More in Common), Patrick Dunne (Boardelta),

Dan Elkes (Transparentem), Hassan Elmasry (ClientEarth), Kate Hampton (Children's Investment Fund Foundation), Tirana Hassan (Human Rights Watch), Richard Hawkes (British Asian Trust), Leslie Johnson (Laudes Foundation), Olivia Leland (Co-Impact), Ed Marcum (Working Capital), Lawrence Mendenhall (AAO), Gemma Mortensen (New Constellations), Sonal Sachdev Patel (GMSP Foundation), Minh-Thu Pham (Project Starling), Jonathan Prentice (IOM), Eloise Todd (Pandemic Action Network), Maran Turner (Freedom Now), Mabel van Oranje (Girls Not Brides, VOW for Girls), and Dan Viederman (Working Capital). My additional thanks to Dan Vexler and Maria Horning, as well as Sarah, Tim, Brendan, Mabel, Sonal, and Natasha (Dolby), for reviewing all or part of the manuscript and offering insightful feedback. And my heartfelt thanks to my dear friends Brad Haynes and Simone Burford for their friendship and moral support throughout.

I learned a lot from the two bosses I worked for during my nine years with International Crisis Group, Gareth Evans and Louise Arbour—some of it recounted in these pages. I also benefited from the wisdom of many wonderful colleagues at that truly impactful organization and made many lasting friendships. Together with the Freedom Fund, it's the organization I've most enjoyed working for in my decades of professional life. My former Crisis Group colleagues are too numerous to list here, so I'll limit myself to thanking my former bosses on behalf of all of them.

I have received significant encouragement and support for this project from the partners at Legatum, one of the Freedom Fund's cofounders. The partners—Christopher Chandler, Mark Stoleson, and Philip Vassiliou, as well as Alan McCormick—have an abiding interest in leadership and have been enthusiastic champions of this book from its inception. And, of course, it was their decision to partner with fellow philanthropists Andrew and Nicola Forrest and Pam and Pierre Omidyar that brought the Freedom Fund into being—for which they all have my everlasting thanks.

This book became much more real when Matt Holt Books agreed to publish it. I'm very grateful to Matt Holt, editor in chief, for his faith in me, a first-time author, and this project. (I'm also awed by his encyclopedic knowledge of obscure Australian movies.) And to Katie Dickman, managing editor, whose thoughtful and skillful editing significantly enhanced the final text.

My thanks to Mojie Crigler, who provided me invaluable advice on how to go about writing a book proposal and pitch it to publishers. She also provided lots of editorial support throughout, particularly in the early stages when I was still working out how to actually write a book.

Erin Phelps, my senior adviser at the Freedom Fund, very kindly helped with a lot of the research. She also provided valuable input and guidance throughout and, in particular, offered helpful perspectives on issues ranging from impact to DEI. The book is much the better for her input.

I get a great deal of support and joy working with my senior leadership team colleagues at the Freedom Fund. They are all outstanding leaders in their own right. They contribute greatly to the quality of my leadership, ensuring the organization benefits from better and wiser decisions than I could make on my own. I owe a particular debt of gratitude to Dan Vexler, our managing director for programs and my longstanding friend, who stepped in as a highly effective interim CEO while I was on sabbatical. He was ably supported by the rest of the team: Zoe Marshall, managing director for finance and administration; Amy Rahe, managing director for external relations; and Havovi Wadia, director of programs. My deep thanks to all of you.

And finally, I want to thank all of my colleagues at the Freedom Fund, past and present. From our modest beginnings, we are a team of eighty-two in twelve countries at the time of writing, and our collective work is impacting millions of lives. I have learned so much from working with this team over the years. Much of what I've shared in this book comes very directly from my experiences at the Freedom Fund. Certainly, it's been a collective effort to build an inclusive and impact-focused culture and a powerfully effective organization. I've benefited greatly from the commitment and expertise of all those I've worked with at the Freedom Fund. My huge gratitude to all of you.

NOTES

PURPOSE: SET THE DIRECTION

1. Malala Yousafzai is a Pakistani activist for girls' education and recipient of the Nobel Peace Prize in 2014. This quote is from a speech she made at Harvard in September 2013.
2. Leeuwin Ocean Adventure Annual Information Statement 2022, Australian Charities and Not-For-Profits Commission website, accessed July 1, 2023, https://www.acnc.gov.au/charity/charities/4bc9d964 -38af-e811-a961-000d3ad24182/documents/3fbf8abc-f171-ed11-81ac -002248110683.
3. Dina Sherif, email to author, December 2022.

CHAPTER 1: MISSION

1. From a speech the Indian leader (Mahatma) Mohandas Karamchand Gandhi gave on October 31, 1938, at Dera Ismail Khan, India.
2. "How We Work," International Crisis Group website, accessed May 15, 2023, https://www.crisisgroup.org/independent-impartial-inclusive.
3. Rebecca Hamilton, *Fighting for Darfur: Public Action and the Struggle to Stop Genocide* (London: St Martin's Press, 2011), 121.
4. "The International Crisis Group and the ENOUGH Project: A Complementary Relationship," International Crisis Group website,

May 4, 2007, www.crisisgroup.org/who-we-are/crisis-group-updates/international-crisis-group-and-enough-project-complementary-relationship.

5. "Vision and Mission," Grameen Bank website, https://grameenbank.org.bd/about/vision-mission.

6. "Facts About Girl Scouts," Girl Scouts website, accessed February 13, 2023, www.girlscouts.org/en/footer/faq/facts.html.

7. "About Us," EDWINS website, accessed May 25, 2023, edwinsrestaurant.org/about-us/; see also Ed Pilkington, "Inside the Restaurant Serving Up Second Chances for Ex-prisoners," *Guardian*, November 26, 2019.

8. Homepage, More in Common website, accessed February 13, 2023, www.moreincommon.com.

9. Peter F. Drucker, *Managing the Non-Profit Organization: Principles and Practices* (New York: HarperCollins 1990), 3; see also William Meehan III and Kim Jonker, *Engine of Impact: Essentials of Strategic Leadership in the Nonprofit Sector* (Stanford: Stanford Business Books, 2017), 27.

CHAPTER 2: IMPACT

1. Jim Collins is a leading researcher and author on business leadership. One of his best-known books is *Good to Great: Why Some Companies Make the Leap and Others Don't* (New York: Harper Business, 2001). This quote comes from his monograph on nonprofits titled *Good to Great and the Social Sectors* (London, England: Random House Business Books, 2006).

2. "Delivering So Much More Than a Meal," Meals on Wheels America website, accessed February 13, 2023, www.mealsonwheelsamerica.org/learn-more/what-we-deliver.

3. "Impact Report 2019," Change.org website, accessed February 13, 2023, static.change.org/brand-pages/impact/reports/2020/2020_Impact+Report_Change_EN_final.pdf.

4. "Our Impact," Heritage Foundation website, accessed February 13, 2023, www.heritage.org/our-impact.

5. "Our Story," Ali Forney website, accessed February 13, 2023, www
   .aliforneycenter.org/our-story.

6. "Free Distribution or Cost Sharing? Evidence from a Malaria Prevention Experiment in Kenya," *Quarterly Journal of Economics*, February
   2010, www.povertyactionlab.org/sites/default/files/research-paper/83
   %20Dupas%20Q JE.pdf.

7. "Tracking spending on cash transfer programming in a humanitarian context," Development Initiatives, March 2012, devinit.org/wp
   -content/uploads/2012/03/cash-transfer-financing-final.pdf.

8. Dylan Matthews, "A Charity Dropped a Massive Stimulus Package
   on Rural Kenya—and Transformed the Economy," *Vox*, November 25, 2019, www.vox.com/future-perfect/2019/11/25/20973151
   /givedirectly-basic-income-kenya-study-stimulus; see also "Uncon-
   ditional Handouts Benefit Recipients—and Their Neighbours Too,"
   Economist, November 23, 2019, www.economist.com/middle-east-and
   -africa/2019/11/23/unconditional-handouts-benefit-recipients-and
   -their-neighbours-too.

9. "Cash Transfers Help Pakistan's Poorest," World Bank website, May
   19, 2016, https://www.worldbank.org/en/results/2016/05/19/cash
   -transfers-help-pakistans-poorest.

10. "World Bank Signs $400 Million Project to Protect India's Poor and
    Vulnerable from the Impact of COVID-19," World Bank website,
    December 16, 2020, www.worldbank.org/en/news/press-release/2020
    /12/16/world-bank-signs-usd400-million-project-to-protect-india
    -s-poor-and-vulnerable-from-the-impact-of-covid-19.

11. Ugo Gentilini, Mohamed Almenfi, Ian Orton, and Pamela Dale,
    "Social Protection and Jobs Responses to COVID-19: A Real-Time
    Review of Country Measures," World Bank website, April 17, 2020,
    openknowledge.worldbank.org/handle/10986/33635.

12. This quote is often attributed to Albert Einstein, but it appears the
    correct source is sociologist William Bruce Cameron in his 1963 text
    Informal Sociology: A Casual Introduction to Sociological Thinking (New
    York: Random House, 1963).

13. "Unlocking What Works: How Community-Based Interventions Are Ending Bonded Labour in India," Freedom Fund website, September 2019, freedomfund.org/wp-content/uploads/Freedom-Fund-Evidence -in-Practice-Paper-Unlocking-what-works.pdf.

14. Ken Roth, email exchange with author, August 28, 2022.

15. Collins, *Good to Great and the Social Sectors*, 8.

16. L. Becker, J. Wolf, and R. Levine, "Measuring Commitment to Health: Global Health Indicators Working Group Consultation Report" (Washington, DC: Center for Global Development, 2006).

17. Arthur C. Brooks, "AEI's President on Measuring the Impact of Ideas," *Harvard Business Review*, March–April 2018, https://hbr.org /2018/03/aeis-president-on-measuring-the-impact-of-ideas.

18. Dan Vexler, "What Exactly Do We Mean by Systems?" *Stanford Social Impact Review*, June 22, 2017, https://ssir.org/articles/entry/what _exactly_do_we_mean_by_systems.

19. Nick Grono, "How Measuring Systems Change Can Open the Door to Transformative Impact," *Center for Effective Philanthropy* blog, January 2023, https://cep.org/how-measuring-systems-change-can-open -the-door-to-transformative-impact/.

CHAPTER 3: STRATEGY

1. John Lewis Gaddis is Lovett Professor of Military and Naval History at Yale University. This quote is from his book *On Grand Strategy* (New York: Penguin Press, 2018).

2. Wendy Kopp's senior thesis at Princeton University, as recounted in Sarah Thorp (2000), *Teach For America*, HBS 9-300-084, hbsp.harvard .edu/cases/. See also Bill George, Diana Mayer, and Andrew N. McLean (2007), *Wendy Kopp and Teach For America* (A), HBS 9-406- 125, hbsp.harvard.edu/cases/.

3. Thorp, *Teach For America*, 7; also Wendy Kopp interview, "Creating an Education Leadership Movement with Teach For All," *System Cata- lysts* podcast, July 4, 2023, https://www.systemcatalysts.com/episodes /creating-an-education-leadership-movement-with-teach-for-all.

4. Michael Brown of City Year, quoted in Collins, *Good to Great and the Social Sectors*, 16.

5. Thorp, *Teach For America*, 9; George et al., *Wendy Kopp and Teach For America* (A), 5; Bill George, Diana Mayer, and Andrew N. McLean (2007), *Wendy Kopp and Teach For America* (B), HBS 9-407-031, hbsp.harvard.edu/cases/.

6. Wendy Kopp, "Criticism Toward Teach For America Is Misplaced," *Washington Post*, September 18, 2014.

7. "Our Impact," Teach For America website, https://www.teachforamerica.org/what-we-do/our-impact, accessed May 30, 2023.

8. President Dwight Eisenhower, "Remarks at the National Defense Executive Reserve Conference," November 14, 1957, https://www.presidency.ucsb.edu/documents/remarks-the-national-defense-executive-reserve-conference.

9. Patrick Dunne, "From a Maps to Satnav World—The Way Boards Take Decisions Is Changing," LinkedIn, September 28, 2021, www.linkedin.com/pulse/from-maps-satnav-world-way-boards-take-decisions-changing-dunne/.

10. Susan Colby, Nan Stone, and Paul Carttar, "Zeroing In on Impact," *Stanford Social Innovation Review*, Fall 2004, https://ssir.org/articles/entry/zeroing_in_on_impact.

11. "What Can Scaling Organizations Learn from Teach For America? It All Starts with Your Theory of Change," Bellwether, February 5, 2015, https://bellwether.org/blog/what-can-scaling-organizations-learn-from-teach-for-america-it-all-starts-with-your-theory-of-change-3/.

PEOPLE: BUILD THE ORGANIZATION

1. Reid Hoffman is the cofounder of LinkedIn. This quote is from the book he coauthored with Ben Casnocha, *The Start-Up of You: Adapt to the Future, Invest in Yourself, and Transform Your Career* (New York: Currency, 2012).

CHAPTER 4: THE CEO

1. Mary Parker Follett was a leading leadership thinker and writer in the early decades of the last century. This quote is from her 1924 book, *Creative Experience*.
2. Email to author, September 26, 2022.
3. Cited by Collins, *Good to Great and the Social Sectors*, 10.
4. Françoise Moudouthe, email to author, November 15, 2022.
5. Daniel Goleman, "Leadership That Gets Results," *Harvard Business Review*, March–April 2000, https://hbr.org/2000/03/leadership-that -gets-results.
6. Goleman, "Leadership That Gets Results."
7. Greg Mortenson, *Three Cups of Tea* (New York: Penguin Books, 2006); see also Jon Krakauer, "3000 Cups of Deceit," *Medium*, July 21, 2014, https://medium.com/galleys/greg-mortenson-disgraced-author -of-three-cups-of-tea-believes-he-will-have-the-last-laugh-760949b1f 964#.gbzin9b4t.
8. Mortenson published a follow-up book, *From Stones into Schools*, in 2009, which was also widely promoted by him and CAI. See Montana Attorney General's Investigative Report of Greg Mortenson and Central Asia Institute, Office of Consumer Protection Montana Department of Justice, April 2012, accessed June 20, 2023, https://web.archive .org/web/20121027082246/https://files.doj.mt.gov/wp-content /uploads/2012_0405_FINAL-REPORT-FOR-DISTRIBUTION .pdf.
9. "The . . . scene in Korphe about building a school happened in September 1994, a year later," according to Greg Mortenson, quoted in Alex Heard, "Greg Mortenson Speaks," *Outside*, April 13, 2011, https:// www.outsideonline.com/adventure-travel/destinations/asia/greg -mortenson-speaks/; see also Jon Krakauer, "3000 Cups of Deceit."
10. "Questions over Greg Mortenson's Stories," *60 Minutes*, CBS News, April 19, 2011.
11. "Questions over Greg Mortenson's Stories," *60 Minutes*; and Kevin Sieff, "Mortenson Returns to Afghanistan, Trying to Move Past His 'Three Cups of Tea' Disgrace," *Washington Post*, October 12, 2014.

12. Montana Attorney General's Report.

13. Nicholas Kristof, "'Three Cups of Tea,' Spilled," *New York Times*, April 20, 2011, https://www.nytimes.com/2011/04/21/opinion/21kristof .html.

14. Sieff, "Mortenson Returns to Afghanistan, Trying to Move Past His 'Three Cups of Tea' Disgrace."

15. Montana Attorney General's Report, 13.

16. Peter Hessler, "What Mortenson Got Wrong," *New Yorker*, April 21, 2011, https://www.newyorker.com/news/news-desk/what-mortenson -got-wrong.

17. Herminia Ibarra and Anne Scoular, "The Leader as Coach," *Harvard Business Review*, November–December 2019, https://hbr.org/2019/11 /the-leader-as-coach.

18. Goleman, "Leadership That Gets Results."

19. Goleman, "Leadership That Gets Results"; see also Ibarra and Scoular, "The Leader as Coach."

20. T. J. Saporito, "It's Time to Acknowledge CEO Loneliness," *Harvard Business Review*, February 15, 2012, https://hbr.org/2012/02/its-time -to-acknowledge-ceo-lo.

21. Marc A. Feigen, Michael Jenkins, and Anton Warendh, "Is It Time to Consider Co-CEOs?" *Harvard Business Review*, July–August 2022, https://hbr.org/2022/07/is-it-time-to-consider-co-ceos.

CHAPTER 5: THE TEAM

1. Doris Kearns Goodwin is a renowned historian of US presidential leadership. This quote comes from a speech to Pittsburgh Arts and Lectures on October 28, 2019.

2. See 2020 Top Foreign Policy and International Affairs Think Tanks (Table 19) in James G. McGann, "2020 Global Go To Think Tank Index Report" (2021), TTCSP Global Go To Think Tank Index Reports, 166.

3. Wale Odunsi, "International Crisis Group Appoints Nigeria's Comfort Ero as President," *Daily Post*, December 24, 2021,

dailypost.ng/2021/12/24/international-crisis-group-appoints -nigerias-comfort-ero-as-president/.

4. Bryan Walker and Sarah A. Soule, "Changing Company Culture Requires a Movement, Not a Mandate," *Harvard Business Review,* June 20, 2017, https://hbr.org/2017/06/changing-company-culture-requires -a-movement-not-a-mandate.

5. Michael D. Watkins, "What Is Organizational Culture? And Why Should We Care?" *Harvard Business Review,* May 15, 2013, https:// hbr.org/2013/05/what-is-organizational-culture.

6. Jennifer Howard-Grenville, Brooke Lahneman, and Simon Pek, "Organizational Culture as a Tool for Change," *Stanford Social Innovation Review,* Summer 2020, https://ssir.org/articles/entry /organizational_culture_as_a_tool_for_change.

7. Boris Groysberg, Jeremiah Lee, Jesse Price et al., "The Leader's Guide to Corporate Culture," *Harvard Business Review,* January–February 2018, https://hbr.org/2018/01/the-leaders-guide-to-corporate-culture.

8. Specifically, the "value" of their companies. John R. Graham, Campbell R. Harvey, Jillian Popadak, and Shivaram Rajgopal, "Corporate Culture: Evidence from the Field," National Bureau of Economic Research, March 2017, www.nber.org/papers/w23255.

9. Howard-Grenville et al., "Organizational Culture as a Tool for Change."

10. Donald Sull, Charles Sull, and Ben Zweig, "Toxic Culture Is Driving the Great Resignation," *MIT Sloan Management Review,* January 11, 2022, sloanreview.mit.edu/article/toxic-culture-is-driving-the-great -resignation/.

11. Brittany Levine Beckman, *Mashable,* June 12, 2020, https://mashable .com/article/crisis-text-line-ceo-ousted-nancy-lublin.

12. On Mercy Corp. Mike Baker, *New York Times,* May 9, 2021, https:// www.nytimes.com/2021/05/19/us/mercy-corps-abuse-investigation .html.

13. On Women Deliver. Sonia Elks, Reuters, June 18, 2020, https://www .reuters.com/article/us-global-aid-racism-trfn/top-womens-rights -group-probes-claims-of-racism-by-staff-idUSKBN23P25Y.

14. Rob Preston, Civil Society Media, June 17, 2022, www.civilsociety .co.uk/news/bullying-culture-and-toxic-urge-to-protect-the-brand -found-at-amnesty-international-uk-in-racism-inquiry.html#sthash .8uu5Ffyg.dpuf.

15. Colum Lynch and Shabtai Gold, Devex, November 24, 2022, https:// www.devex.com/news/review-slams-culture-of-fear-potential-fraud -other-failings-at-unops-104521.

16. BBC, March 8, 2018, https://www.bbc.com/news/uk-43324754.

17. Zack Colman, *Politico*, November 12, 2020, https://www.politico .com/news/2020/11/12/audubon-society-claims-intimidation-threats -436215; see also Jeremy P. Jacobs, *E&E News*, "Can Audubon's New CEO Detoxify Its Workplace?," November 22, 2021, https://www .eenews.net/articles/can-audubons-new-ceo-detoxify-its-workplace/.

18. C. O'Reilly and Jennifer Chatman, "Culture as Social Control: Corporations, Cults and Commitment," in *Research in Organizational Behavior*, Vol. 18, eds. B. M. Staw and L. L. Cummings (Greenwich, CT: JAI Press, 1996): 166, cited in Donald Sull, Charles Sull, and Andrew Chamberlain, "Measuring Culture in Leading Companies," *MIT Sloan Management Review*, June 24, 2019.

19. D. Sull et al., "Measuring Culture."

20. D. Sull et al., "Measuring Culture."

21. "Guide: Understand Team Effectiveness," on Google's website, accessed February 12, 2023, at https://rework.withgoogle.com/print /guides/5721312655835136/.

22. This example draws on the "Guide: Understand Team Effectiveness"; Charles Duhigg, "What Google Learned from Its Quest to Build the Perfect Team," *New York Times Magazine*, February 25, 2016, and Charles Duhigg, *Smarter, Faster, Better: The Secrets of Being Productive* (London: Random House Books, 2016), 42–46.

23. Amy Edmondson, "Psychological Safety and Learning Behavior in Work Teams," *Administrative Science Quarterly*, Vol. 44, No. 2 (June 1999), 350–383, https://doi.org/10.2307/26669.

24. Amy Edmondson, "How Fearless Organizations Succeed," *Strategy + Business*, November 14, 2018, https://www.strategy-business.com/article/How-Fearless-Organizations-Succeed.

25. Edmondson, "Psychological Safety and Learning Behavior in Work Teams," 356.

26. Collins, *Good to Great and the Social Sectors*, 13.

27. Peter Cappelli, "Your Approach to Hiring Is All Wrong," *Harvard Business Review*, May–June 2019, https://hbr.org/2019/05/your-approach-to-hiring-is-all-wrong.

28. Lazlo Block, "Here's Google's Secret to Hiring the Best People," *Wired*, April 7, 2015, https://wired.com/2015/04/hire-like-google/.

29. Shawn Achor, Andrew Reece, Gabriella Rosen Kellerman, and Alexi Robichaux, "9 Out of 10 People Are Willing to Earn Less Money to Do More-Meaningful Work," *Harvard Business Review*, November 6, 2018, hbr.org/2018/11/9-out-of-10-people-are-willing-to-earn-less-money-to-do-more-meaningful-work.

30. Edward Deci, "Effects of Externally Mediated Rewards on Intrinsic Motivation," 1971, *Journal of Personality and Social Psychology*, 18(1), 105–115; see also Delia O'Hara, "The Intrinsic Motivation of Richard Ryan and Edward Deci," American Psychological Association website, December 18, 2017, https://www.apa.org/members/content/intrinsic-motivation.

31. Courtney E. Ackerman, "Self Determination Theory and How It Explains Motivation," PositivePsychology.com, June 21, 2018, https://positivepsychology.com/self-determination-theory/; see also Susan Fowler, "What Maslow's Hierarchy Won't Tell You About Motivation," *Harvard Business Review*, November 26, 2014, https://hbr.org/2014/11/what-maslows-hierarchy-wont-tell-you-about-motivation. Sometimes the theory is reframed as "autonomy, mastery and purpose," e.g., Daniel Pink, *Drive: The Surprising Truth About What Motivates Us* (London: Canongate Books, 2011).

CHAPTER 6: DIVERSITY, EQUITY, AND INCLUSION

1. Audre Lorde was an American writer, poet, feminist, and activist. This quote is from a collection of her writings published in her book *Sister Outsider* (Berkeley, CA: Crossing Press, 1984).
2. "A Brief Primer on Diversity, Equity and Inclusion for Nonprofits," Mission Met website, https://www.missionmet.com/blog/a-brief -primer-on-diversity-equity-and-inclusion-for-nonprofits.
3. Asif Shaikh, interview with author, December 13, 2022.
4. Tina Vásquez, "Guttmacher Institute Staff Say a 'Toxic' Work Culture Has the Reproductive Rights Research Giant in a 'Death Spiral,'" *Prism*, December 6, 2021, https://prismreports.org/2021/12/06/guttmacher -institute-staff-say-a-toxic-work-culture-has-the-reproductive-rights -research-giant-in-a-death-spiral/; see also Ryan Grim, "Elephant in the Zoom: Meltdowns Have Brought Progressive Advocacy Groups to a Standstill at a Critical Moment in World History," *Intercept*, June 13, 2022, theintercept.com/2022/06/13/progressive-organizing -infighting-callout-culture/.
5. Colleen Flaherty, "Who's Doing the Heavy Lifting in Terms of Diversity and Inclusion Work?" *Inside Higher Ed*, June 3, 2019, https://www .insidehighered.com/news/2019/06/04/whos-doing-heavy-lifting -terms-diversity-and-inclusion-work; Holly Corbett, "The New Unpaid Office Housework for Women: Being DEI Leaders," *Forbes*, September 28, 2021, https://www.forbes.com/sites/hollycorbett/2021/09/28 /the-new-unpaid-office-housework-for-women-being-dei-leaders/?sh =4cc027db56e8; and Jennifer Miller, "Their Bosses Asked Them to Lead Diversity Reviews. Guess Why," *New York Times*, October 12, 2020, https://www.nytimes.com/2020/10/12/business/corporate-diversity -black-employees.html.
6. Grim, "Elephant in the Zoom."

CHAPTER 7: THE BOARD

1. Anne Wallestad is the former CEO of BoardSource, a globally recognized nonprofit focused on strengthening nonprofit board leadership.

This quote is from her article "The Four Principles of Purpose-Driven Board Leadership," *Stanford Social Innovation Review*, March 10, 2021, https://ssir.org/articles/entry/the_four_principles_of_purpose _driven_board_leadership.

2. "History," International Crisis Group website, accessed May 10, 2023, https://www.crisisgroup.org/who-we-are/history.

3. Patrick Dunne, *Boards: A Practical Perspective*, 2nd ed. (London: Governance Publishing & Information Services Ltd., 2021), 6.

4. Barbara E. Taylor, Richard P. Chait, and Thomas P. Holland, "The New Work of the Nonprofit Board," *Harvard Business Review*, September–October 1996, https://hbr.org/1996/09/the-new-work-of -the-nonprofit-board.

5. Julie Bosman, Matt Stevens, and Jonah Engel Bromwich, "Humane Society C.E.O. Resigns Amid Sexual Harassment Allegations," *New York Times*, February 2, 2018, https://www.nytimes.com/2018/02/02 /us/humane-society-ceo-sexual-harassment-.html.

6. Ian Kullgren, "Female Employees Allege Culture of Sexual Harassment at Humane Society," *Politico*, January 30, 2018, https://www .politico.com/magazine/story/2018/01/30/humane-society-sexual -harassment-allegations-investigation-216553.

7. Marc Gunther, "Accountability? Not at the Humane Society of the US," *Nonprofit Chronicles*, https://nonprofitchronicles.com/2019/03/18 /accountability-not-at-the-humane-society-of-the-us/. (Press release quoted from article, as the release is no longer available on Humane Society website.)

PARTNERS: MOBILIZE EXTERNAL STAKEHOLDERS

1. Helen Keller was an American advocate and activist for the blind. This quote is referred to in the book by Joseph P. Lash, *Helen and Teacher: The Story of Helen Keller and Anne Sullivan Macy* (Arlington, VA: American Foundation for the Blind, 1981), among other sources.

2. The first Global Slavery Index was published by Walk Free in 2013. The most recent edition was published in May 2023. See Global

Slavery Index, Walk Free website, accessed May 31, 2023, https://www.walkfree.org/global-slavery-index/.

CHAPTER 8: THE PEOPLE AND COMMUNITIES YOU SERVE

1. This quote is from Dr. Martin Luther King's sermon "Three Dimensions of a Complete Life," published in the 1963 collection of his works *Strength to Love* (Boston: Beacon Press, 1963).
2. "Statement of Nadia Murad Basee Taha to the United Nations Security Council," Freedom Fund website, December 18, 2015, www.freedomfund.org/blog/5380/.
3. Vibhuti Ramachandran, "Critical Reflections on Raid and Rescue Operations in New Delhi," Open Democracy, November 25, 2017, www.opendemocracy.net/en/beyond-trafficking-and-slavery/critical-reflections-on-raid-and-rescue-operations-in-new-delhi/.
4. Kimberly Waters, "Beyond 'Raid and Rescue': Time to Acknowledge the Damage Being Done," openDemocracy, November 27, 2017, https://www.opendemocracy.net/en/beyond-trafficking-and-slavery/beyond-raid-and-rescue-time-to-acknowledge-damage-being-done/.
5. Dhananjayan Sriskandarajah, "Oxfam Failed Horribly on Abuse. But I Pledge to Deliver Radical Change," *Guardian*, June 14, 2019, www.theguardian.com/commentisfree/2019/jun/14/oxfam-abuse-power-safeguarding.
6. Sophie Otiende, email to author, November 15, 2022.
7. Sophie Otiende, email to author, November 15, 2022.
8. "Advocacy: About Habitat's Advocacy Efforts," Habitat for Humanity website, accessed February 11, 2023, https://www.habitat.org/about/advocacy.
9. "Policy and Advocacy," March of Dimes website, accessed February 11, 2023, /www.marchofdimes.org/our-work/policy-advocacy.
10. "Our Focus," World Vision website, accessed February 11, 2023, worldvisionadvocacy.org.

CHAPTER 9: FUNDERS

1. MacKenzie Scott is a US philanthropist who has given away $14 billion to over 1,600 nonprofits by early 2023. This quote is from her blog post "384 Ways to Help," *Medium*, December 15, 2020, mackenzie-scott.medium.com/384-ways-to-help-45d0b9ac6ad8.

2. Yield Giving website, accessed May 30, 2023, https://yieldgiving.com/.

3. "Understanding How Donors Make Giving Decisions," Lilly Family School of Philanthropy website, January 2022, scholarworks.iupui.edu/bitstream/handle/1805/27562/UnderstandingHowDonors2022.pdf.

4. "Understanding How Donors Make Giving Decisions," Lilly website.

5. Email to author, September 23, 2022.

6. Email with More in Common cofounder Tim Dixon, June 26, 2023.

7. MacKenzie Scott, "Seeding by Ceding," *Medium*, June 15, 2021, mackenzie-scott.medium.com/seeding-by-ceding-ea6de642bf.

8. Michael Sanders and Francesca Tamma, "The Science Behind Why People Give Money to Charity," *Guardian*, March 23, 2015, https://www.theguardian.com/voluntary-sector-network/2015/mar/23/the-science-behind-why-people-give-money-to-charity.

9. Marshall Ganz, "Why Stories Matter," Middlebury College website, March 2009, sites.middlebury.edu/organize/files/2014/08/Ganz_WhyStoriesMatter_2009.pdf.

10. Jennifer Lentfer, "Yes, Charities Want to Make an Impact. But Poverty Porn Is Not the Way to Do It," *Guardian*, January 12, 2018, www.theguardian.com/voluntary-sector-network/2018/jan/12/charities-stop-poverty-porn-fundraising-ed-sheeran-comic-relief.

11. Charitable Giving Statistic, National Philanthropic Trust website, accessed May 30, 2023, https://www.nptrust.org/philanthropic-resources/charitable-giving-statistics/.

12. Nonprofit Impact Matters infographic, National Council of Nonprofits website, accessed May 30, 2023, https://www.nonprofitimpactmatters.org/site/assets/files/1015/nonprofit-impact-matters-infographic-sept-2019.pdf.

13. Alex Marshall, "Museums Cut Ties with Sacklers as Outrage over Opioid Crisis Grows," *New York Times*, March 25, 2019, https://www

.nytimes.com/2019/03/25/arts/design/sackler-museums-donations
-oxycontin.html.

14. William Wallis, "National Portrait Gallery Ends BP Sponsorship Under Pressure from Activists," *Financial Times*, February 22, 2022, https://www.ft.com/content/c3ab1b10-ee06-4fac-abe9-1a1e4dcef39f.

15. FRIDA website, accessed March 4, 2023, youngfeministfund.org/wp -content/uploads/2020/08/RME-1.pdf.

16. Nicola Slawson, "Jo Cox Charity Fund Passes £500,000 Target in a Day," *Guardian*, June 18, 2016, https://www.theguardian.com /uk-news/2016/jun/18/jo-cox-gofundme-royal-voluntary-service -hope-not-hate-white-helmets.

CHAPTER 10: PEER ORGANIZATIONS AND NETWORKS

1. Frederick Douglass was an American abolitionist and former slave. This quote is from his 1855 lecture "The Anti-Slavery Movement."

2. About Child Marriage, Girls Not Brides website, accessed May 30, 2023, https://www.girlsnotbrides.org/about-child-marriage/.

3. Child and Forced Marriage, United Nations Human Rights website, accessed May 30, 2023, https://www.ohchr.org/en/women/child-and -forced-marriage-including-humanitarian-settings.

4. About Child Marriage, Girls Not Brides website.

5. About Us, Girls Not Brides website, accessed May 1, 2023, https:// www.girlsnotbrides.org/about-us/.

6. Mabel van Oranje, email with author, February 14, 2023.

7. "Michelle Obama, Melinda French Gates, and Amal Clooney Announce Collaboration to Support Adolescent Girls' Education and Help End Child Marriage," October 25, 2022, Obama Foundation website, https://www.obama.org/updates/michelle-obama-melinda -french-gates-and-amal-clooney-announce-collaboration-to-support -adolescent-girls-education-and-help-end-child-marriage/#:~:text =Obama%2C%20Ms.,to%20reach%20their%20full%20potential.

8. About, Justice Action Network Foundation, accessed June 30, 2023, www.janfound.org/mission. The Justice Action Network is now the home website for the Coalition.

9. Darren Walker, "A Critical Cause, an Unlikely Coalition," Ford Foundation website, February 19, 2015, https://www.fordfoundation.org /news-and stories/stories/posts/a-critical-cause-an-unlikely-coalition/.

10. Darren Walker, "A Critical Cause, an Unlikely Coalition."

11. Ellen Martin, "Evolving Our Understanding of Backbone Organizations," FSG website, December 11, 2012, https://www.fsg.org/blog /evolving-our-understanding-backbone-organizations/.

12. Laurent Fabius, French Minister of Foreign Affairs and International Development. This account of Crisis Action's work in CAR draws on its 2013/2014 Annual Report and "Creative Coalitions: A Handbook for Change," published by Crisis Action and accessed on March 15, 2023.

ABOUT THE AUTHOR

Photo by Ivan Weiss

Nick Grono has decades of experience leading and chairing nonprofits. He is the CEO of the Freedom Fund, a highly successful philanthropic fund dedicated to ending modern slavery around the world. He serves on a number of nonprofit boards and acts as adviser to many nonprofit CEOs. Nick has written for the *New York Times*, the *Guardian*, and various other publications.